White Stones
Bones
and
Mist
Authentic Movement and living Prayer

Jan Alexandra Sandman

Editing, Design, and Composition by Sarla V. J. Matsumura

Library of Congress Control Number: 2016918577

ISBN-13: 978-0692781487

ISBN-10: 069278148

Published by Lady of the Lake Press

Montpelier, Vermont

DEDICATION

*This book is my prayer. It was written from
an ongoing surge of energy in me that
needed to find expression.*

Dedicated to all life

.

CONTENTS

Preface   i

Introduction   1

The Beginning   18

Stones, Bones, and Mist   22

Authentic Movement Begins   24

The Flower of Life   28

Mover and Witness   31

Silence, Space, Interiority   34

Inner Witness   38

The Great Privilege of Witnessing   41

Breath as Inner Witness   46

The Nature of the Collective Body   49

The Presence of the Other   51

Experimentation and the Power of Intention   52

The Silks   59

Embodied Prayer   71

Offerings   71

Objects   75

Tracking   76

Projections   79

The Signature   81

Northeast Kingdom   84

Transition   87

Prayer   88

Living Authentically   94

Beginnings   111

Action   116

Mystery   117

Holding the Inner Stillness   120

Patterns   122

The Goodness of Patterns, the Goodness of Rhythm   126

Holy Woman, Holy Man   129

Helpers from the Unseen World   131

Simple Joyful Living   133

The Mist: Bridging the Two Worlds—Returning with Your Treasure   135

Speaking, Language, Giving Voice   140

Holiness, Prayer, and Softness   145

Direct Knowing   146

Softness   147

And the White Stones   148

Acknowledgments

About the Author

Preface

For many children, the flow of grace present in the safe womb before birth, safely born and cradled in the arms and at the bosom of Mother, the wise and cooing embrace of Grandmother, the blessing of Godmother, arms and grounded blessing of Father, Grandfather, Godfather, and the lullabies, soft swaddling of clothing and blankets, precious tender stories, soft beloved toys, and movements into the world carried; then toddled and walked gently beside our parental guide; is the last innocence of purity, light, faith, hope and embodied love in which one fully believes as life itself. From this point on, as we scar, we address life as that which is beyond innocence, or is in spite of the naïveté of innocence. We address the sophisticated life as the story of our scars, the dangers of the path of life, that which fails, is heartbroken, or is grasped at to pay us back for the unfairness and suffering beyond the innocent, infantile nature of the moment, day or brief chapter that were a promise of Heaven on Earth in our souls, hearts and lives, once upon a time.

Jan Sandman has created a life embodying this principle of being, of innocence realized, of a living universal faith and practice, and of love toward the sacred in all and among all, in her own private life as an individual, her life within family of origin, marriage, mothering, as therapist, practitioner, teacher, neighbor, colleague, woman, human being. She embodies the practice of the safe birthing of innocence as life itself, each moment, that one might breathe each breath in a holiness of sincere, faithful movement into action of true goodness, essential for the remembrance and realization of all that is holy, real and good among us all, within all of creation, beside all of life, honoring. East Indian sage Sri Aurobindo called this *the Life Divine*, grace moving from Heaven through breath, each cell, into all that is.

Jan has dreamt for some years of scribing into book form her work in movement that it might serve as a signature, an emblem, an example, and as a primer for others; that, just as she moves from the void of meditative breath, prayer, and contemplation through the whiteness of all light, into all colors of light and yet one, and through the sounds, music, fabrics, instruments and spaces of her practice and teaching into the streams, covered bridges, mountain byways and forests, ponds and lakes of her home in Vermont and throughout our world , her soul moves in her great heart and love, in the words of beloved poet Rainer Maria Rilke's memorial adage:

> Quiet friend of many distances, feel
> How your breath still enlarges space.
> Let yourself ring out, a dark cradled bell
> In the timbering. That, which erodes you
> Gains a strength from your sustenance.
> Go out and in, though transformation.
> What is your experience of greatest loss?
> Is drinking bitter, then become wine.
>
> Be, in this night made of excess,
> The magic art at the crossroads of your senses
> The sense of their strange encounter.
>
> And if the earthbound forget you,
> Say to the silent Earth: I flow
> To the rushing water say: I am.
> Sonnets to Orpheus II.29
Translation A.S. Kline

Elizabeth Anne Hin
December 2016

Introduction

Authentic Movement is part of the bedrock of my life. I have practiced and taught the form for many years and what I have found is that for me, it is a form that holds, allows, and promotes growth, change, and life itself. As I change and grow as a human being, I have never had to abandon the form. It allows me to become more of who I am in all ways and still practice with full integrity. The form teaches one to become more truly and fully themselves.

Authentic Movement is a practice that developed in the 1950's through Mary Starks Whitehouse, a student of Martha Graham and Mary Wigman. Mary Starks Whitehouse, a professional dancer and psychotherapist, with an interest in Jungian principles, gave birth to this form, calling it Movement in Depth. Her combination of dance and psychotherapy was the beginning of dance movement therapy. Janet Adler, who was influenced by Mary Starks Whitehouse, coined the term Authentic Movement and continued to deeply develop the work in her own direction. Now, the work has flowered in many directions.

The essence of the form involves a mover or a group of movers who move with closed eyes, listening and acting from the inner impulse of the body. The movements emerge from the body rather than the mind or the intellect. A non-judgmental witness observes and creates a psychic, energetic, and spiritual container for the movers. The importance of being witnessed, being seen, is key to the development of the inner witness of the participant. The work crosses boundaries of psychology, creativity, body wisdom, spirituality, and more.

It is interesting to notice who finds Authentic Movement appealing. I have noticed that the people who are drawn to the form seem to have in common that they are kinesthetically based and that they enjoy being in an open-ended conversation of exploration with their bodies, hearts, minds, and spirits. I have found that the form works best with people who have a strong enough container of self that when they descend into the open-endedness of the Authentic Movement form, their predominant feeling is not one of overwhelm. In the group setting, movers and witnesses are open to each other and to many subtle energies. To be able to hold one's own boundary with the inner witness, while allowing the flow of the group energies and the dissolution of armoring to happen, allows the experience to be a positive one or opportunity for growth.

I have been practicing this form since 1991. I studied with Janet Adler in the 1990's. I have studied deeply with two long standing groups: one that has been meeting monthly for 25 years and the other that has been meeting yearly for two decades. Both of these groups have been invaluable to me in the study and practice of the form.

I began teaching the form about twenty years ago and have allowed the teaching to evolve with my own inner evolution. This book has arisen out of this history of moving, practicing, and teaching. Over the years, I have led groups that have been very traditional Authentic Movement groups to very experimental groups. I continue leading groups and practicing in all ways, both traditionally and experimentally. For me, all forms are necessary and valuable for helping me deepen my understanding and insight into the form and into the nature of human beings.

In the groups that are what I would name traditional, there is nothing from the outside imposed upon the group. We have stripped away any outer influence. The mover is alone with him or herself and nothing more. It is as though one is standing solitary in an open landscape. The sounds come from the inside, the movements and visions come from the deep interior. It is a very pure practice of the self in relationship with the self.

In the groups that have included other aspects that I call in, for example, the energy of Color, the elements of Nature, spirituality, embodied prayer, I am using the form as a means to explore something in particular although I have no expectation about where the work will go. It becomes a different kind of collective experience as there is a joining, a holding, and a teaching through the pieces I have called forward. The bond becomes quite strong and through it, the collective moves as one in a particular way. When working with embodied prayer as a focus, a universal prayer is generated. Interestingly, this happens also in the non-focused groups, but in a different manner. I am studying this.

As a leader, facilitator, and witness of this work, I receive so much. In part, what I receive is the great privilege of studying embodied consciousness. To study and witness people as they work at their depth, in an inner trust in earnest and profound conversation with themselves and their own guidance is a gift beyond all words. All the people who have practiced the form with me are stars in my heart. Each person, along with the priceless gift of their movement, is an unspeakable treasure. After each group, I often thank the participants for coming, for offering what they do. I am completely sincere in this. I feel that each movement circle helps each other and helps the world in its own way. It is through my groups and the people who create them that I have been able to learn and practice and explore in this form and I am eternally grateful for this.

Although the photographs in this book have been taken with one particular group moving with colors through silk, I want to stress that all of the groups I work with, whether we are including the colors and silks or not, embody the deep principles presented here. In the writing of the book, it was simply necessary for me to choose a focus in order to accomplish this written work.

I wish to note that although this book focuses on the practice of Authentic Movement as a means for guiding one to live a deep spiritually based life, the principles, many of the examples, and the depth of presence and witnessing as guiding forces in awareness are not unique to Authentic Movement. Many spiritual traditions as well as movement and embodiment practices and practices of daily living and work attend to the principles I speak of in this book. What I speak of here can be universally applied to anyone's life, whether they practice this form or another, or no named form at all. For example, the writing applies in principle to many forms of embodiment and consciousness training and practice: Aikido, Somatic Embodiment Training, Contact Improvisation, Awareness Through the Body to name a few. In addition, a Buddhist, a Christian, a Jew, an artist, a musician, a baker, a teacher, a businessperson could all relate to the principles of attention, listening, and presence presented here. The principles can be universally applied to anyone's life, perhaps bringing forward a deeper, richer experience of living.

White Stones, Bones and Mist

I bow my head

to all who have come before me

to all who will come after me

my hands spread on the basket's reeds

The opening is before me

My gratitude pours in

I prepare the space

The colors are speaking to me

coming alive

the atmosphere is sparkling with light

We are getting ready to receive what will be given,

what will be offered, what will be moved.

The colors

each themselves

my hands

placed

on the Turquoise silk,

through that to the earth

Turquoise silk connected to all the silks in their serpentine shape

The path they take

as we begin

My prayers are for protection

Deep connection

Deep answers

My hands press down

I feel heaven and earth meeting me here

in this moment, this place

Now

The prayers are taken

They are received

We are ready

Center is the place that is found

the edges of the veil are stripped off

opened

the heart's prayer is named

The objects wait

holding space while

movers descend into the place where

boundaries shift

where time shows its true face

Turquoise rises to the heights

and descends to the depths.

A single finger points the way

in the apex of light.

The Beginning

In the mid 1980's, my father was diagnosed with tracheal cancer. By the time it was diagnosed, the cancer was at a very advanced stage. Henry Joseph Sandman identified himself as a German man and was very proud of it. Of all the things he could have called himself, an equestrian, an athlete, a scientist, a humanitarian, he chose to always let me know that he was German. After his death, I discovered that he was also Irish, English, Scandinavian, and possibly not German at all. Were these ancestral lines not mentioned or just not known? Would it have changed his feeling about himself to be with his fullness? Why did he want me to know that he was German, and yet I would have to pull from him feelings about being an equestrian? What we own and what we do not own about ourselves is curious.

My father was a strong man in ways that we don't typically think of as strength. He was defined by alcohol for all the years that I knew him. The alcoholism contributed to him dying early, at 64, but without the alcohol, perhaps his life would have been unhappier. He was strong in the way of generosity, love of people, faith in people. He had a longing for the goodness in humankind to prevail, and a mysterious sadness that it just could not be so. Every instance of human kindness was so precious to him, it would move him to tears.

My brother Jay later took up that sentiment to a much greater degree as he also took up alcoholism to a much greater degree. The recognition of the good in people always came as a desired but unexpected gift and it was always followed by tremendous sadness of knowing that this is always possible but so rarely lived. And in that way, kindness was a bit of a torment, bringing longing and tears to the foreground.

For a time, I was the youngest child. At 6, I became the middle child. I revered my older brother, Jay, and adored my younger brother, Jon. I grew up in freedom: spacious, airy New England woods, dappled by sunlight.

Birches, oaks, maples, pines, ferns, mosses, lady slippers. I spent most of my free days in the forest, alone or with friends, communing, being, wandering, leaving early in the morning and returning later in the day. Building forts, making stews out of plants, collecting rocks, admiring mosses. In my back yard, a Grandmother Willow lived. She was my guardian Spirit Tree. In good times and bad, I would go to her for connection, consolation, advice. Her rough bark, her climbable branches, her long droopy hair all held me in a profound comfort. To stand in summer, in the green space created by her weeping branches, was to enter a world of my own. I could feel within her the steadiness of the world. She had a sizable knot in her trunk at about eye level. There was a tiny imperfection in the knot that served as a door knob. Through this knot, I would stand and gain entry to the tree. I would energetically be taken in to the world of the Willow, traveling up the branches to the higher regions of the tree, in close communion then with sky. I would remain there, in a perfect union, completely at rest. She spoke a language that I heard and understood. It was not words as we know them, but very slow sound. I could perceive from the Willow a promise of a kind of unshakable unity.

I was told that I lived in my imagination. To me it seemed I was simply living, connecting many worlds, inner and outer, one foot here, one here, one here—the world a blending of the inner and the outer. I do not strongly differentiate the inner and the outer worlds. I see and feel how they blend, how they talk and relate with each other. In the way that my father and brother were spiritual beings with intense unrequited love for God, Spirit, Humanity, I am living a life of what feels like satisfied love, deep love, realized love.

This book tells some of that journey. Authentic Movement as a pathway to authentic living is a huge contributor to that.

The White Stones: Tracheal Cancer. He is living alone with my mother, in his late fifties. She would call me, "There's something wrong with your father. He's just not right. It's like he's a very old man. He can hardly walk. He won't go to the doctor. I am worried about him." Her complaints are not frequent, but are serious, grave. Finally, my father, Henry Joseph, agrees to an appointment, but on that very day, collapses bleeding from the mouth. He is taken to the hospital, where he is given a death sentence and a diagnosis. His world spins out of control. My mother is shell-shocked and I am pulled into an ocean of grief. Both my life and his pass before my heart. He has been such a strong influence in my life, inspiring and terrifying, dreaded and loved. How could he be dying? Aren't we just beginning to get on an even keel? Wait, Dad. Are you going to die without finding peace in your life? Can this be it? It's so incomplete, so full of holes and errors and misunderstandings.

My heart streams with raw, red hot grief. How can I let you go? How can I help Mom live beyond you? I am at the beach, Cape Cod, walking the beaches, miles and miles. The days are sunny, there is wind. The surf pounds its rhythm, over and over. This is completely essential and yet also is merely the backdrop for me. The container for me. I am crying, walking and crying, walking and crying. The salt of the ocean could be fueling my tears, ocean water rising up through me and out of my eyes. I am collecting Stones:

White Stones, grieving stones, each stone, a round white nugget of the unspeakable pain. I know that somehow the stones are essential, they are helpers, I need them with me. These white round beings, washed and washed in the cold Atlantic waters. I choose them carefully, they are choosing me, "Take me," they say, "take me and me and me." They fill my pockets, my towel, my bag. White Stones. Grieving stones. Friends. Helpers. Perhaps it is their color, how they stand out against the wet dark sand, how they stand out against all the other stones. Perhaps it is the hours I spent as a child with the stones from the forest, knowing them inside and out. As a child, I took my collected rocks, and with a hammer, I smashed them open, to reveal their hidden beauty, their deep crystalline shine. What I learned is that no matter how much I opened the stone, it was its own new world. Center is everywhere. The infinite shows itself to me.

From Cape Cod, I take the stones home, each one its own world, each one an example of the infinite, of what goes on and on without end. I set them in bowls, beautiful copper bowls inlaid with turquoise enamel. I love them. I just keep loving them. They help me.

My father receives intense radiation. He outlives his diagnosis; he becomes a medical marvel, he is written up in medical journals. He is alive but not well, never again strong. My mother strains to care for him, she cannot stand the thought of him dying, she cannot bear that thought. My mother, while caring for him, dies first. She is 62. A year and a half later, on their wedding anniversary, my father dies at age 64. I am devastated by these losses, in an indescribable whirlwind of loss and grief. Three weeks later, my daughter enters my life through the miracle of adoption. It is 1989. I move from death to birth.

I pour my love into life. I pour it and pour it. Life.

Now my brother, Jay, has taken the family torch of despair. It has reached into his body; addictions have taken him over; it has reached into his spirit; he talks constantly of depression and suicide. I am his sister; I am here with life; but I am also there with him, with death, with despair, with hopelessness.

I have a foot in this world and that world, one reality and another, both real, both important. I am ecstatically happy as a Mother, I am in despair as a sister. I want to help, I want to change things for others, for him, I cannot. But I try and I try and I try. I cannot. I am the one who must learn how to love a deep sorrowful path all the way into death. I am the one who must learn not to go down with the ship.

At this time, I had a bodywork practice, centered in mind, body, spirit connection.

I begin the study and practice of Authentic Movement.

Stones, Bones, and Mist

Stones: My white bones of the earth. Stones consolidate their energy, their shape, the elements they are formed from. Stones hold the history of the earth in a committed, longstanding, and communicative way. Stones come to me from outside of me and connect me with worlds beyond myself. They will be here long after I am gone.

Bones: Inner structure. What holds me up, gives me shape, forms me. My bones help me to be this and not that. They give me definition. I have worked for my bones, worked to find the right bones that can support my particular body, my particular spirit, my particular soul work in the world.

My bones include my family, my deep friends, ceremony and prayer, the life and work of Elizabeth Hin, all of my teachers, color, sound, nature, Authentic Movement, my daily work.

When I find a new bone, it is a momentous occasion, for I integrate the new bone into my structure and of course, everything has to shift, rearrange, make room for this new supporting element. Eventually, it becomes part of me in a way that is as natural as breath.

Mist: Mist goes in between. Ethereal and light, mist connects, surrounds, envelopes. Mist is here then not here. Mists conceals then reveals then conceals again. Mist is not held or contained. It is the opposite of the stone. Mist expands and travels world to world to world, ineffable and silent.

Each one informs me. Bones, stones and mist: the outer, the inner, and the in-between. How they work together, how I listen to the conversation between all three is how I know my way.

The stones are representative of how the outer world speaks to me, informs me, holds me. I say stones and I mean all elements of the outer world: the mountains, the lakes and rivers and oceans, the trees, and plant world, the species of animals that come and go, the sky and stars. The outer world is here without me. It is here before me and after me. And yet, as I am here, I am a welcomed part of it. I am included. I am not alone.

My bones are the history I come from, as a person, as a soul and the tools and structures I assimilate along the way that feel so correct that they become a part of me. They are my skeleton. Without any one of them, something would be incomplete. I am more upright, more myself, because of them. They are the people, places, energies that have formed me, taught me, held me, worked with me. All of them have been necessary, all of them a gift. I welcome them into me. I am not alone.

The mist dances in all the in-between places. Mysterious, ineffable, yet profoundly present. I am a traveler of the mists, aware and listening into what cannot be grasped, but can be observed and felt and known in the non-grasping state. In what I call the mist, I encounter many beings, teachers, wise ones, and experiences of ecstatic flow. It is here that I encountered the beings I named the Angels of the In-Between, it is here that my teaching from the Flower of Life occurs, it is here that many important formative and transformative transmissions occur for me.

The book named itself. It was here before any of the writing began. It was here years before the writing began, as though it was waiting for its story to be told.

Authentic Movement Begins

I am walking through downtown Montpelier, Vermont. It is the early 1990's. I notice a flyer posted on the window of Bear Pond Books. An intriguing Chinese brushstroke-like graphic of an image that is moving in many directions is in the center. The image suggests great space, possibility, and freedom to me. The words on the flyer say Authentic Movement. The description speaks of body, curiosity, and mystery. I have never heard of Authentic Movement. I know I must try it.

This is my beginning, my first time. There are about ten people in the workshop. Sara Norton, an Aikido master, Tai Chi teacher, and psychotherapist is leading the circle. She gives us clear yet mysterious instructions about closing our eyes and moving from the inner impulse, about entering the unknown. I am ready.

She sounds the bell that marks the beginning. I hear this sound for the first time. It rings and cuts the air. It rings and resonates out into space. It rings and silence follows. It rings and I am brought to a gentle attention in myself. All circles I have ever been in begin and end with the sound of the bell. I have no idea then that I will hear this same sound thousands of times more. And that each time I hear it, it will mark the beginning or the end of something deep, truthful, and unique.

I close my eyes. My body comes alive. My hearing intensifies. My sense of space and the ability to perceive through my physicality heightens. I stretch. The space around me feels huge and vast. Am I alone?

No, I am not. I can hear the others, I can sense them. I begin to wonder what they are doing. But then I am taken over by an urge to get low to the ground. I squat down. I am perched there, low to the ground. The others around me are becoming more distant, almost muffled, as my attention is pulled to the feeling that something is in front of me. It is palpable and ineffable both at once. My heart is beating strongly. I reach my hands out to touch it, to find out what it is. Suddenly I am filled with emotion, love, and sadness. It is my friend, who has recently died. She is here. No, I am there, with her. I am on the road where she crashed, I am with her. I am stroking her forehead. I am saying thank you, I am saying goodbye. She is going now. The energy is receding. Her brown hair, with its shock of white, her petite strong body, her muscled arms, her serious and kind face. She is receding. And I am alone in the space without her. The sounds of the other movers begin to return as though a veil had come down around me protecting me from their sounds and now the veil has lifted. I am back with them. I lie down on my back, filled with emotion, filled with the experience.

The bell rings. The session is over. I have closed my eyes and entered other worlds. I know I belong here with this form.

And now decades later:

It is necessary to open my eyes now. Now. No exclamation point. Period. It is time to see, write, listen, and record what must be said. I have been practicing now for close to 25 years. Authentic Movement is one of my Bones, is part of my skeletal structure. It is woven into the fabric of how I live. I deeply trust it. For me, this path allows me a form of endless permission to dive into truth, crossing many borders of mind, body, and spirit. I experience the form as limitless. A landscape that leads to the deep centered richness.

We all have a place of deep center. For me, I experience it as an inner sanctuary, residing in the region of my heart, but not my heart. It is connected to a vertical axis, that connects heaven and earth. I have developed my connection with it over time. For each of us, it is different. Some of us live from the place of deep center. Some of us dip into it. Some of us skirt around it. When we are in it, we are supported and nourished by it. For me, this deep spirit place is god or godlike. Here we can listen to, interface with, and at times become a direct channel of or manifestation of this clear energy.

This clear energy is in motion, moving with a direct knowing momentum. For me, it moves with a place of no question, pure knowing, no impediments. Clear energy, deep center, direct knowing, the god within us all, completely *Hearted*, loving and knowing.

The Flower of Life

Intricate, infinite, symmetrical,
ordered, moving, pulsing, alive
conscious oneness, eternal,
existing somehow in all things
at all times each infinite point,
another doorway of knowing.
Question and answer resolved
in oneness, always.

As I first sat to write this book, powerful energy inundated me. I would write a page or two and then my writing would be stopped as my mind was taken over by a powerful surge. I would simply sit with the energy, integrating, listening deeply. It was like listening to the sound of the planets spinning, audible in the most remote region of hearing. Over time, the energy revealed itself as the Flower of Life. Its influence and teaching has stayed with me for the duration of this writing.

The Flower of Life is a living shape of sacred geometry. Much has been written about it that can be easily accessed. In a pearl, its significance lies in the understanding that it is connected to all of life, all knowing, that all of life is connected. The quality of this connection is infinite, opening out and out into eternity. All knowing is within it, or of it. It is found in almost every religion in one form or another. No one originated it, it simply is. All of the other sacred geometric shapes are contained within it. The Tree of Life is contained within it, the Seed of Life is contained within it as is the secret shape called the Fruit of Life.

The Flower of Life was revealed to me as a transmission in an altered dream state about 20 years ago. At that time, I did not know its name but was brought mystically into the remembrance of the consciousness that it is. It is very meaningful to me that the energy of the shape has appeared to accompany me through this writing. At different times, depending upon what I am writing, the Flower of Life illuminates and emanates energy, pulses as I am writing. I feel guided by it and honored to be with the experience so closely. So often in this book I am writing of the connectedness of all things, the infinite nature of things, the eternal pulse. I believe that is why the Flower of Life is with me so strongly—to allow that to come through.

Authentic Movement directs a person inwardly to develop trust with that pure inner place that has no bounds, no limits. It does so through the vehicle of the body. The body, though temporal, is fingerprinted with the infinite mark of the eternal throughout. As physical forms, we become increasingly light as our bodies extend out past the initial density. Everything you see opens out, opens out, opens out, infinitely, like the Flower of Life. Alternatively, in our physical forms, everything also opens in, opens in, opens in, infinitely.

We are living mandalas, moving forms of sacred geometry. So as you venture into this book, as you hear me speak about moving in any way, know that the movement I name, or the movement that is seen or felt, is but the visible point of an infinite continuum that moves both inwardly and outwardly.

Some of us are connected to our bodies with the sensuous sinew of a cat or the deep grace of the swan or the horse. Some of us are less identified with our bodies. We may be more like the turtle, we have soft innards and an outer shell self. Some of us have a signature where our bodies are a primary vehicle for experiencing the world. Others of us are more mystical or intellectual or practical giving the experience of embodiment a very different lens. Our bodies are shaped differently, fed differently, brought up in different places. We are born here, born there, raised by this person, by that one, in this way, kindly, cruelly, fed enough, fed too much, not enough, rich, poor, alone, connected, brothers, sisters, none at all. All of this creates our bodies. Into this, our genetics rise up, who we came from, who we descend from. We are all descendants of someone else. We owe our very lives to others, no matter who they are, how they treated us or each other, how they failed us or didn't, we owe our lives to others. We have a history as a soul. Who we have been in past lives impacts certain aspects of this life.

Then there is our personal history, what we have created and or chosen with our free will and our destiny in its complex and beautiful dance. We all have a destiny. The destiny is the path of action that connects the soul's journey to the flower of life, to God in Creation, however you might name that for yourself: the Divine, the Tao, Creation, The Center, the Heart, Nature.

Mover and Witness

In the form of Authentic Movement, there are two basic elements: the Mover and the Witness. The relationship between the two is what gives the form its potency. The witness consciousness

(non-judgmental presence) is held by an outer witness (another person) as the Inner Witness (the mover's ability to observe without judgment) develops over time and with practice. The Mover's work is with eyes closed, in the presence of the Witness, tuning into the ever-changing and evolving impulses of the body and allowing their expression through movement. To let the body lead. To listen to that wisdom. We can move pieces that are connected or expressive of any aspect of our soul's journey. Our bodies latch onto a thread. The thread itself is potent. It may be a thread we have touched and worked with many times before, or it may be a new thread. The threads are mysteriously wired into this entity we call a body. The body is physical, temporal, and related to the physical world.

In Authentic Movement, we can move from solidity to the numinous. We can begin with what is solid, what is formed, what we can sense through our senses. We can begin as though the body is a wise teacher, a place of vast beginnings with a unique, singular, and pure sense of things. We can begin from a place that is not thought-generated, that is not from the mind, but tapping into a mysterious place of another way of knowing. When we access a clear sense of embodiment, we are in direct connection with the physical plane of ourselves, all people, all animals, all trees, all aspects of nature, the planet, and even the cosmos. Through this, because as movers we are resonating on the physical levels as well as on other less dense levels, we can affect and move clear energy that can help in the deep energetic and spiritual balancing that our world so deeply needs. The physical levels resonate with each other and through the physical connection, the less dense energies are also transmitted.

For example, as I bring prayer into my heart and I am connecting fully with as much transparency as possible, the energy is moving through the physical plane of the body. As I practice moving with this energy of the prayer, it is resonating on the physical level of existence. Here, it is able to reach and affect things that are also on that level, the level that some may consider to be the densest level of existence. It is as though there is a common language of understanding. This is how we can be an agent of change and deep prayer.

Let's say that my prayer is for the protection and awakening of the children. In my deep center, I feel the prayer. I feel the energy of it, I am one with the prayer. I wait in silence until I am drawn in by the prayer to the movement circle. My eyes are closed, I am connected to the energy of the prayer and I open my body to allow the physical expression to come through. I have no idea what will happen. I am truly trusting my body to be the vessel for the prayer. Invariably, the energy builds up and travels through all my bodies, physical, emotional, mental, etheric, spiritual, causal. So the vibration of the prayer is given access and permission to move through all the realms of human dimension through my body to the highest vibration I am capable of and grounded in the physical world where it resonates out on the physical plane. This requires a deep trust of one's body to let go of control.

Our history and our environment form our bodies. Our bodies are here in the form they are in to work with our soul's destiny. We have the bodies we have as they are correct for how and why we are here. They are packages of personhood, each expressive of a jewel of Creation. How we experience our bodies and through our bodies is a magnificent act of creation, grace, and unlimited trust, unique for each of us.

In Authentic Movement, I invite the darkness, the inclusiveness of Black, the dark, deep interior. As a mover, I begin by closing my eyes. As the eyes close, I eliminate the visual outer world, accentuating and inviting the inner vision to become active. With closed eyes, I amplify my hearing, my sensations, and my relationship to space. Immediately, I am stretched, accessing Trust in new ways as I can no longer see. I don't know where I am in space, in the room, in relationship to others. I don't know who is around me. If someone is touching me, I don't know who it is. I cannot see with my eyes what is happening for them, or within them. I cannot use my visual faculties that could put one in a place of judging or assessing a situation with mind or thought.

As a mover, I must turn then to something else—for balance, for determining safety and risk. Other, less utilized parts of oneself become more awakened.

My ears wake up. I may begin to hear and listen more acutely. This hearing and listening may be outside of me or it may be an interior listening. The experience of outside and inside becomes heightened and sometimes merges. The birds I hear are chirping inside my head. My heartbeat is outside of me in the drumming sound of another mover.

I am now listening inwardly. I listen with my ears and also listen in other ways. I perceive, I discover new ways of perception that have been dormant with eyes open living. Then, when I open my eyes, the open eyes become more conscious, more perceptive, more seeing.

Silence, Space, Interiority

Before anyone enters, I prepare the space. I am gathered into my center, focused completely on what is to come and on what is. I am considering the wholeness of each person in the group, calling them forward energetically saying hello, saying welcome, however you are in this moment: welcome. I am circling the space, moving counterclockwise through the space, in a state of consciousness that I will call a gateway. I circle counterclockwise, to wind down and into the Spirit. I have already left the ordinary world outside the door. I invite and pray for a thinness of the veils that allows deep access to everyone for what they are to move and for what is to come forward and be expressed.

I set up the altar. It may be simple or complex depending upon the group, depending upon the outer circle, the circle of my own soul and the threads or connections that I work with. This is always holding the group. My prayers are holding the group as well as many other things. My White Stones may be there, an ancestor stone from Scotland may be there, a candle, a Coptic cross that was given to me in deep faith for my path. These objects are my mainstays. I have prayed with them for decades and their energy sustains me and the work of the circles.

As I prepare the altar and the space, I walk, circling a path down in for the whole of the group. I ask for protection and mercy for each and every one. I ask for courage. I wait, releasing expectations. I wait in faith for grace to make its appearance in the circle.

The circle is a whole, the circle is an AUM, the circle is a disc, the circle is enclosing, the circle is an opening, the circle is a nest, the circle is a portal. I feel excited, expectant, in the presence of mystery, in awe. I have no power, but I would not call myself powerless. Instead, I would call power irrelevant and faith essential. As a faithful one to the circle, I call my trust forward. I find and feel that I trust the circle, the sense of I AM, the Flower of Life, God. I am a vehicle, a holder of space for the movers who are coming, a holder of space for what must or can be moved and opened. The more open and clear I am, the more the circle can allow, hold, move. There is a relationship. I ask and pray for my eyes and ears and senses and heart to be clear, to see deeply and to see beyond the veil, to be humble in the face of that which I cannot clearly see or understand. The more I practice this form, the more I let go, the more I trust and see and feel this essential life-giving current of life, Flower of Life in operation.

I choose my words carefully when speaking to the group as I know that they are already in an altered state and listening acutely. I am careful with the deep attention they are giving me. It is a gift. I know all words have impact. Each word has a vibration, a history of use and comprehension. Each word is perceived differently by different movers. I know that their movement experience will be shaped by the words I say. I trust the words I speak, the words that emerge when they do. I prepare things to say but often what I say is not coming from prepared thought, rather words are being made available for me to speak in that *Moment*, flowing words. I will use the phrase flowing words rather than channeled words as channeled feels as though it is coming from another being. The only beingness that speaks through me is Creation.

In the Authentic Movement form, I hold a tight structure in all ways except the movement itself. The tight structure allows a safety for the vastness that is and does ensue.

One of the important structures is eye contact. The eyes are the windows of the soul. The eyes are powerful connectors, mirrors, expressers of light, of emotions, of soul energy, of trust of heart, of that which cannot be named but can be directly felt, exchanged, and allowed. As we stand in the circle, readying ourselves to begin, we connect with each person in the circle through eye contact. We exchange a moment of seeing each other and being seen by each other, without words, without it meaning anything other than what it is to purely connect as one being to another. Here we begin to acknowledge and feel the wholeness of the circle. This is a time to attend to and witness with the inner witness any sense of emotional, psychic, or energetic weaponry or shielding that one may have with another person in the group. It is a time to notice, can I make eye contact and still breathe with each person? Are there some people with whom it is more difficult for me to see or be seen by? This would be a place to take note of the inner witness.

Then we turn our attention to the center of the circle. We witness the empty space. The empty space is the great circle. The mystery, the opening, the beginning, the nest. The empty circle is present mystically as we begin, the wholeness. We witness emptiness; we allow emptiness. We allow a moment of that Silence to be there without having to or trying to fill it. We allow Space. We stand there together in silence and space. Space and Silence that is simultaneously both full and empty. The void is before us, complete. Everything is possible, everything is present, the prayers have been made. Anything can happen here, the highest joys, the deepest darkness, and everything else. Simultaneously.

As we witness it out there before us, we are the circle. Holding, seeing, hearing, sensing the great silence and space, I direct people to notice that same spaciousness inside of themselves. The inner world and the outer world in Eternity are one.

What is eternal is outside and inside. As we can connect and maintain connection with that eternal place through sound, vision, breath, we are one. We are now connected as one interwoven being in the space of the eternal. As we begin this journey into the wisdom of our bodies, as we close our eyes and see with our inner eyes, we have the touchstone of eternal oneness, inside and outside within ourselves and among us.

Inner Witness

Many of us have developed a connection to the outer world as a presence that evaluates, scrutinizes, draws conclusions, judges, and takes action based on these things. There is often an inner fear that we are being judged. Most of us have less rather than more connection with a non-judgmental inner presence. When people tune in to themselves, often what they hear is a conversation happening that is censoring, frightened, intimidated, trying to get the upper hand, wondering what others think, wondering how to please, conflicted between two or many different ideas, impulses, thoughts, or feelings. This is not the inner witness but an inner critic or an inner voice.

The true inner witness is perceived in different ways for everyone. There is no one way. Some commonly stated qualities are that the inner witness is a state of being, is vast, is non-judgmental. The inner witness is accepting, limitless, expands wider and wider, and opens deeper and deeper. It has a sense of the cosmic and grand overview or overseer. The inner witness feels like a space of great calm and peace no matter what is happening in the experience as a whole, whether it is calm or emotional or deeply physical. The inner witness observes, witnesses. It is like the eye in the center of the storm. The development of the inner witness is the core of the practice of Authentic Movement.

To move is one thing, to move with awareness and consciousness is something else altogether. The awareness opens something, opens a path of movement really and energetically in both the individual and the collective body.

The individual body is one's own personal space and boundary and life. You are moving from a deeply personal place, your personal history, relationships, issues, emotions, creativity, spirituality, body. To move from the collective body means something different. You are connected energetically to the other movers, to the movement that is happening as a whole in the collective body, to the movement that may be happening in the larger collective, the town, the state, the world, the animals, the trees. The collective to which we all belong. There are many collectives superimposed upon one another, intermingling. To move with the collective is to have a more open boundary, moving deeply in the web of life.

I describe the inner witness often in this manner: To witness something fully is an act of love and consciousness. When you choose to witness, to be in that space of your deepest clarity, you are deeply centered in your own Inner Being. You are not pulled in any direction. If you think of yourself as the universe, you are in the center of it. If you are a flower, you are the center of it. From that space in consciousness, you move. Perhaps you are moving an emotion or a physical pattern or exploration or an image that is strongly with you. As you simultaneously move and witness inwardly, as you move, you are *seeing* this aspect of yourself. As you *see* it you are giving it recognition and validation. You are freeing yourself from identification with it or from being merged with it. You are putting space around it. As that space comes around it, the space is a kind of freedom or choice or expression of the whole, like an encounter with the great void, which is not empty but full.

All possibility lives there in a latent state. When you bring your attention to any one point of this latency, it pulses, it jumps up, it is full of everything. Now are you drawn there? Does your body speak to you there? Pull you there?

As movers and witnesses, we watch for this potency: that mysterious phenomenon of being pulled or drawn to move something. An energy presents itself, calls to you. It may be big or small. You notice it. Your noticing of it while in that state of inner witness allows more space around it. The energy rises up, perhaps gets bigger in your awareness. As you notice it, feeling the draw to it, if you then choose to allow it, trust it, go with it, it is possible you may then feel, in a mysterious way, that you are not alone. It is as though some inner current is with you, accompanying you, working with you, working through you. You give it your consciousness, your witnessing. In actuality, you are giving it energy. The energy is an act of creation. You are allowing something to unfold and be created right in the here and now. Its seed comes from somewhere in the accessible energy field. You caught it through your attention and gave it space to grow and show itself. Now it is moving. If you let go enough, you will actually feel moved by it, as though you are not doing the moving at all but being moved by this. Effortless. Your body, mind, heart, and spirit as one are all there, in there with That.

This space is so rich that it has the quality of Holiness. Reverence. Wholeness.

Often a conversation goes on between these spaces, these leanings and places you are drawn to and the energy that they hold. They are each doorways into an ever-opening flower, experience, place. To move into those places and conversations with the presence of the inner witness is a monument to consciousness.

The Great Privilege of Witnessing

To be a witness is a multifaceted experience and responsibility. You are, first of all, a holder of space. You are the one whose consciousness remains awake and aware so that the movers can descend down into themselves. You are a protector of the circle, the space, a buffer between the day world and the descending and ascending Authentic Movement world. You are the one who sees the profound vulnerability and courage, the rawness and the exploration, the declarations and discoveries, the questions and the uncertainties of the movers. It is a great privilege. As a witness, you are responsible for witnessing not only the movers, but yourself as well. To witness is to hold movers and yourself in a non-judgmental seeing state. As a witness, you are using all of your senses. You are using your whole body as an instrument of perception. Normally as a witness, your eyes are open, looking at the mover or the movers. You allow your eyes to be drawn to movements that have a charge or pull for you while at the same time, you are staying awake and aware of the whole. You are wide in your gaze and focused in your gaze. As a witness, it is not important or even usually possible to understand what the meaning of the movement is. Often what happens is that the witness gains an understanding about themselves through witnessing another. Occasionally, the reflection can be so astute that something that feels like revelation occurs, as though a curtain is being pulled back, the energy becomes rarified, heightened, can feel rather sparkly. I call these moments revelatory and in them feel Divine presence.

As witness, you use all faculties: eyes, ears, senses. You stay present with your inner witness so that you are witnessing yourself as well as the mover. An example of the inner witness and outer witness might go like this:

I see the mover with the blue shawl kneeling in front of another mover. Her head is bowed, her hands wrapped around her holding onto her sides. She is rocking back and forth. The mover who stands above her does not interact, even though the mover with the blue shawl is making small sounds. As a witness, in my own body as I see this, my chest tightens, my belly tightens, my throat tightens and I feel deep sadness. I am reminded of my own childhood and how I often felt unseen. At the same time, I hold a space large enough to encompass the mover with blue shawl. I do not know what she feels, but I hear her small sounds and I see her clutching her sides and I see and feel her rocking.

As you can see, you are witnessing, seeing the mover, noticing details. You do not know what that mover is feeling or what their movement is about. Instead, you notice your own inner workings as you witness both the mover and yourself.

Who is being healed through this, if healing is even the right word? Both the mover and the witness through the seeing and the inner seeing are benefitting from this. Remember when something is seen fully, the act of seeing, of giving your precious energy or consciousness to something creates an increase in energy that facilitates a movement in whatever is trying to be moved or ready to move. The energy has its own direction. It knows how to move if we will only allow it.

Sometimes the mover and witness will become so connected, it is as though the boundary between them literally disappears and they become one. Then there is no separation between the two. In such a state, the witness may actually feel and sense what the mover is experiencing, not as a spectator or an influence from the outside but as an inner experience. They are merged in a unified state. This state is not a merged codependent state, but a finer frequency of the Unified field, of oneness.

Who is mover? Who is Witness?

The deeper one travels into the form of Authentic Movement, the more clear it becomes that the roles of mover and witness are mysteriously interchangeable. As a mover, you are witnessing your Self within yourself and in relationship to your body, mind, heart, and spirit. Your eyes are closed, witnessing the space around you, the other movers, what you see, hear, sense, feel around you. You are witnessing an awareness of the witnesses witnessing you.

As a witness, you are witnessing inwardly and externally, you are allowing an *Inner* movement to occur in an honored and lively way as you are paying attention to the movers and to how they affect you. You are being moved even as you witness.

Witness and mover are now coming closer and closer together. The energy of the circle is strong, the boundaries are soft and solid both at once. The energetic weapons are put down, the defenses are put down in many cases. Because of this, there is an unusual fluidity between each other.

In this fluidity, it is possible for the mover and witness to be having the same experience. And it is possible that two or more movers, intimately joined through deep inner witnessing, deep trust of their own bodies and the currents that are drawing them, deeply trusting themselves and the profound goodness of the moment become immersed in an ecstatic flow of energy and movement that can seem and, I believe, is actually removed from ordinary time and space. Two or more witnesses in their open state of receiving suddenly palpably feel that they are connected, that they are one.

We are in the realm of the sacred, the place where angels sing, where holy winds blow.

The more I practice and teach Authentic Movement, it becomes crystal clear that, at its highest and best, the form is pure ceremony. It is from this purity that I am called to engage with it. As a spiritual practice, a spiritual form. I consider that each series I teach for a certain number of weeks is a ceremonial segment of time and space that we call forward and then release at the conclusion.

I invite the movers to pay attention to bringing objects that relate to what we are moving with, that relate to their inner witness, that relate to something internal that they feel or perceive and externalize that into the earthly world, the earthly realm. This pulls the participants into a deep conversation with a sensate experience of their inner and outer world; an imagistic relationship to their inner and outer world; a thoughtful entering into trying to put a definition in the waking world onto what, if left alone, might remain an untended, unspoken world. Its gifts may slip away. Can we catch them, hold them for one moment to feel the grace before they slip back into the mist?

When the object appears and is chosen and shows up each week on the altar, it begins to take on an energy, in and of itself. It begins to connect with an aspect of the person's intention or soul. Sometimes an object that someone brings is actually important for someone else to see, to behold. It begins to become part of the movement ceremony. What happens to it and with it, where it is placed on the altar, in relationship to what, where it came from, whether it is remembered each week or forgotten, whether it breaks or is lost is important. Whether it retains its meaning for them, or whether the meaning and importance fades. Everything becomes meaningful.

An example of this involves a tiny clear crystal star-like object that one mover began to bring to the altar each week representing an inner aspect of state of being. Before she placed it on the altar, she would hold it carefully between her thumb and forefinger and raise it up in a gesture that to me, allowed the light to come through it, allowed it to symbolically take its place in the heavens, and thirdly emphasized the star-like quality of this person's signature. She would then place it on the black altar cloth where it would emanate its vibration. The wholeness of this gesture and object created an imprint energetically that after awhile belonged not just to the person who brought the crystal star but to the entire group. Even when she was not there, the crystal star came energetically. I would simply hold up my forefinger and thumb in the way that she did and the energy of the crystal star would be present. Her energy would follow. Her imprint was so strongly in the crystal star and the crystal star's energy imprints strongly with the ceremony of the circle, that whether it was physically present or not, it was there. And its imprint resonated out to connect with everyone.

The movement circle begins to expand into the everyday world. What happens in the circle with the intention is now carried out into the day world, the wide awake world, the eyes open world.

My inner intention as a facilitator is of the utmost importance. My inner intention is to bring awareness, trust, and ease to our authentic selves, so that we can live from that place and begin to emanate from there.

Breath as Inner Witness

In some of her teachings, Elizabeth Hin makes reference to what she calls the "realized breath." She speaks of addressing realization through the breath itself. I am drawn to this and begin to consider the idea of the breath as a way to deepen and maintain the relationship with the inner witness.

The conscious breath

The unarmored breath

The breath that has no weapon and no guarding

The breath without shielding.

Breath is an ongoing happening whose relationship to life force, to the physical body, to the physical world, the earth, the trees, the plants, the pulse of life, if remembered, places us in the present moment.

Breath is shared

Breath is abundant

Breath is everywhere

Some might say breath is Creation's nourishment.

Breath connects us to each other, to the past and the future and the present. Breath is the surrounding ocean. It has been shared always. Every being who ever existed has imprinted on the breath we breathe. Every prayer, impulse, thought, emotion is imprinted in the air we breathe and share. Not only the prayers, impulses, thoughts emotions of people, but of everything. As we inhale the nourishment of the Breath Ocean, it penetrates every cell, every living aspect of our bodies. Our bodies in each unfolding moment are the summation of all that we are, all that we ever have been, the vibrating resonance of being. When it is encountered and nourished by the breath, the breath absorbs the resonance of that encounter and whatever is there in that moment is exhaled, released back out into the oceanic pool, now with our imprint.

As people, we are conditioned to stop our breath, often, to a great degree or a small degree. We control our openness and our connection through controlling our breath. We build invisible walls and armoring and weapons through how we are in our breath. When the breath is halted or constricted, life force is also constricted. If I am holding my breath when I encounter someone in the day world, or another mover in the circle, I cannot feel them, as I cannot feel myself. So rather than there being a flow between us, where holiness can move there is instead a wall. The wall is constructed simply by holding the breath. Now we are separate. I do not feel the other person or myself. Now there is other rather than oneness. Duality.

There is a perception now of danger. The other can harm me, in a big way or more likely a small subtle way. So rather than allowing that, I may harm the other first. It can be as simple as pretending that I didn't hear something that they said or as blatant as pushing my way in front of someone in a line as I consider myself to be more important than another. In so doing, I am also using a weapon against myself.

My breath is your breath. God rides on the breath. When we stop it, we stop that connection, that possibility, that nourishment.

In Authentic Movement, I offer an invitation to pay deep attention to the breath. I encourage each mover to allow the breath its fullness no matter what is happening, to allow the breath to meet the movement fully. As the breath fully meets each movement, each gesture, each emotion, and impulse, the awareness is enormous.

We allow the breath itself to be the inner witness. The breath with its constancy, compassion, life giving qualities:

> "Allow the breath to sit quietly with you and next to you and in you whether you are joyful or scared or curious or exuberant or fast or slow or big or small. Listen with your attention and feel the breath meeting you where you are. Feel its soothing presence, its awareness, your awareness, its affirmation of life. The breath flows in and out. It is not static. It comes and goes, returns again and again until you leave your body. The breath is a connector and a connection. It shows us the living pulse of unarmored life, weaponless life. As you allow breath to be your inner witness and breath to be unarmored, you notice your armoring, your defense, and the opportunity to soften it."

In the circle through breath, the pulse of life is experienced, the cosmos is experienced, the extent to which trauma still holds is experienced. Breath is in direct relationship to embodiment. Authentic Movement brings primary focus to the body as the vehicle for everything: the prayer, the idea, the release, the insight, the exploration, the shamanic connection, the spiritual ecstasy, the emotional dive. The breath accelerates and amplifies the consciousness of all of this. To be present and inside and with that breath as these experiences occur amplifies the understanding of the deep capacity of what is possible through a life lived. A Living Life. The vast beings that we are. The enormous capacity of what we are capable of no matter what. It is not difficult or complicated.

The Nature of the Collective Body

In the form of Authentic Movement, there is the sense that everything can come into correct relationship. Conflicts can find their way to resolution. Disparities within the self and between members in the group and between outer beings or entities can be resolved or realized by coming into correct relationship.

If we consider the circle, the whole, the round body, it has no beginning and no end. It encloses, it rolls, it is a whole, a hole and doorway, a mouth, a cave, a container. The circle in this case is the space formed by a circle of many movers. It is the space in time and consciousness that we have designated for practicing this form, inviting the unconscious, or unseen, or unmanifest to come forward through the body.

We work on the perception and premise that the circle is whole, invites wholeness and can contain and hold all parts, all pieces, all aspects. We work on the premise that all of you can show up and when there is witnessing, things come into correct relationship with the whole. For example, if I have a strong interior experience of shame or grief that is hidden, unacknowledged, it becomes very dense and tight and withheld.

If this grief or shame is offered the spaciousness of witnessing, space then surrounds it. Consciousness is spacious. This witnessing presence offers the grief or the shame, or whatever is being witnessed, space. Literally more room. In this spaciousness, what needed to move, now can move. It is freed from constriction. Now, movement and breath bring what was out of balance into correct relationship with the individual and with the whole circle.

If a mover has a need to do strong, quick, or noisy movements and another mover finds these movements to be overwhelming or invasive or *too much*, is one mover right and one wrong? No. If both movers are being true to themselves, being authentic, then there is something being addressed and worked with in the circle. The circle will move it.

If one mover grieves deeply and another mover or witness has difficulty hearing, seeing, being with the grief, it is an opportunity for that mover to address the authenticity of this feeling that they find to be difficult and to enter into relationship with that in themselves. If one mover must make sound and another mover must have quiet, and is bothered by the sound, one is not wrong. To enter into relationship with that which you find difficult is to come to a new place with it in yourself. The circle holds that.

Perhaps today I am the one who grieves, tomorrow it will be you, and the next day a third person. Today I am moving anger, tomorrow it will be you, and I will be singing. Everything is fluid. We all hold a place and move what is to be moved in the circle.

When we are working with collective energies, we are also working with what is beyond the circle. It may not be my pain, but the earth's pain, or every woman's pain. It may not be my grief, but the grief of a starving nation. It may not be my rage, but the rage of millions oppressed.

Hold it, recognize what it is without needing to define it, and move it through your body. Trust your body to know what to do and how to move it.

The Presence of the Other

It is not uncommon, while practicing the form, for participants to have experiences with conscious energies. These energies may be ancestors, animal spirits, nature spirits, spirit guides, beings from other realms, or deities. It has always been my experience that these energies happen in a way that is natural for the mover and in a way that can be integrated.

I consider it a gift, for example, when a whale shows up to move with me. Or the Color Blue appears to move with me. I, personally, have had a number of deep inner teachers show up on the inner planes to work with me over a period of time. They would appear when I began to move and I received instruction from them regarding particular bodies of knowledge that they had. I would integrate the knowledge through the movement of my body, where it would go directly into my cellular memory.

One such teacher is the Wolf. I had a dream while in an Authentic Movement retreat, regarding my ancestors and family relationships. One of the ancestors handed me a gift that I thought was a fur hat. As I marveled and turned the hat in my hand it was revealed to me that it was not a hat at all, but a living head of a wolf. The dream was startling and lucid. I took the dream directly into movement, embodying the gestures I was using in the dream to hold the wolf's head. Just as with the crystal star object I spoke of earlier, when I held my hands in the dream gesture, the wolf's head appeared. I moved with the Wolf energy then in an incredible intimate extremely slow dance of communion. The entire time, the wolf was instructing me, showing me, leading me. I was following. During this movement, I was receiving a direct transmission from the wolf on Wolf's way of being and Wolf wisdom. My entire brain, nervous system, way of perceiving the world was forever changed by that movement. My vision, hearing, sense of smell, and kinesthetic sense all became very heightened and remained in that state for quite a number of years.

Experimentation and the Power of Intention

Many years ago, in the late 1990's, in what feels now like another era, I had a significant dream. In the dream, I was practicing in an Authentic Movement circle, with a group of people who I regularly moved with at the time. The circle was energetic, active, and intense. At one point, I heard an inner voice tell me, "Open your eyes, you must open your eyes." I did. To open the eyes in the circle is an extreme action that brings the conscious world to the unconscious or mystery world. This would normally not be done.

What I understood this dream to mean is that it was time and of importance in the world to begin to bring the power of what happens in Authentic Movement, what it is capable of, out into the needs of the wide awake world. The dream was telling me that the work is so powerful and the world in such need, that the contribution of the psychological and spiritual integrity should not be kept sheltered, but made intentional, with eyes open. It was imperative to expand the principles and possibilities into the eyes-open world.

I made a commitment with myself to let go of constraints and to allow my intuition to have free reign within the structure and form of Authentic Movement. At the time, I was working with a group of women, many of whom I am still working with, and I asked them if they could agree to that. They agreed and experimentation with the form was born.

I began slowly, deeply trusting and listening to my intuition, bringing in concepts and principles for the group to focus on and move with. These were relatively small at first, but a departure from the wide openness of a normal Authentic Movement group with no focus. Typically, a *traditional* (if there is such a thing) group has no focus, but is wide open to whatever direction each individual member takes it. What I began to do was to introduce ideas and practices of bringing in energies to feel and move with aspects of the human dimension: Fear, Armoring, and Openheartedness.

To facilitate this exploration, I first introduced movement with elements of the natural world: Trees, Elements, Crystals, and Animals. I invited participants to expand the sense of individual boundary by actively inviting in these energies to learn from them directly. We explored direct transmission through Trees, the Elements, Crystals, Animals, Plants and much more. When something is called into the circle and the circle is in ceremony, it is possible to connect with what is directly called in, then to move with it through your body and cells. Once the Element or the Animal is called in, the spirit of it is there to move within the circle. It is not a thinking process, an intellectual process. The form of Authentic Movement prevails, but we have invited in another energy, another mover so to speak.

For example, in calling forward the spirit and energy of Horse, for one person this could facilitate a personal healing. She moves and remembers her own horses; she remembers falling from them and breaking bones. She remembers how her life changed. She feels grief old and deep as she moves. She feels the presence of her particular horse there with her.

Another mover does not feel a particular horse, but instead the overarching energy of Horse; Horse as a force or a teacher; Horse showing something about how to move differently, how to be in the body differently. Or the horse might be needing something from the mover, either a single horse or the energy of Horse altogether. It is necessary for the movers to stay wide open to their experiences and the presence of whatever has been summoned.

Through introducing the energy of ceremony into the classes, I was entering into my own conversation and deep trust of my relationship with the Divine to hold and guide me as the facilitator of the work. Authentic Movement has become my platform, vehicle for doing the work I do, which is on very vast levels, and also deeply personal in guiding people to uncover, develop, and trust their truest selves. I invite the movers to pay more and more attention to details: to the objects they bring, how they relate to what we are moving with, to their inner witness, to something internal that they perceive, trusting how the outer world speaks, how the world we have created around ourselves, who we live with, what we love, what we use, where we go, what we do is the Holy Story we are looking for. This invites the participants into a deep conversation with a sensate experience of their lives.

The objects are offered each week, creating the altar. The prayers and imprints are there from each person in and with the objects. The objects are present for the movement, absorbing the vibration and resonance we are working with each week. They go home, and are present in the participants home environment throughout the week, continuing to resonate the vibration from the circle, continuing to remind the participant of the inner witness, of the ceremony. The movement circle has now expanded into the everyday world. What happened in the circle with the intention is now carried out into the day world, the wide awake world, the eyes open world. The events of the everyday life are included in the ceremony. It is all one. The day itself begins to take on a holy quality not just for me, but for each of the movers—a day marked for depth, reconnection, and rekindling the authentic threads.

I am deeply connected to the spiritual work, teachings, and beauty of Elizabeth Hin of the White Rose Foundation. She is my colleague, my friend, and my teacher. One year, while I was at a retreat she was leading at Asilomar in California, I had the insight during one of the meditations to take the essence of her words and teaching and to bring them to an embodiment through Authentic Movement.

I began to work with those principles. Whatever the focus of her class was, I sifted through the principles she was laying out and translated them into questions that the group could explore and embody through movement. The depth of the group and work solidified around each person as they began to have an experimental form to really work with their own deep inner structures, inner teachers, spirituality, with what has formed them, what is important, listening and trusting and moving from that point. Deeply trusting the unknown, God, mystery.

Season after season, year after year, the odyssey continued. I began to work differently, using the form to call in the Colors, to work with the energy of pure color vibration. I began to create long pieces of dyed silk that hold the energy of the color in a pure way. I brought these silks to the movement circle and invited people to dress in conjunction with the color so as to saturate the space with that color. I invited people to tune into and feel the colors, to experience what it is to be instructed, cradled, and moved by the subtlety of color vibration.

This work with the Colors brought me deeply into my own way of being with the world, which is primarily through subtle vibration. When I work with the Colors, I feel deep relief as I trust their purity implicitly. To me, they are living vibrations that both form us, form the world and cosmos as well as having the property to instruct us and guide us and balance us. They are deeply related to sound vibration and through the Colors, sound can be accessed as well. An essential part of me lives here with this. It is Holy Ground. I am never away from it. I find it to be saturated with love. To have found a way to work with the Colors and sounds is a profound gift to me from the heavens. The idea came to me through a trusted friend who simply said to me one day, "Why don't you work with Color—that would suit you, be in alignment with who you are."

This was a revelation and a point of my soul saying, "Yes, of course." Then the means simply revealed themselves through the silk and the dyes.

I began in a basic way, through the spectrum, working with each basic color. Then I began a year and a quarter long series moving through Black, Dark colors, Light colors, White, Starlight. These series with the Colors have been life changing for me and for many of the people who participated in them.

The process of making the Colors has become a beautiful conversation between the color and the work of the series and the group. I heat a big pot of water to boiling into which I put the dye, sometimes a lot, sometimes just a touch. I stir and stir the yardage of silk, sometimes for five minutes, sometimes for thirty minutes, until it is exactly right. When the colors appear on the silk, if they are *right*, my entire body relaxes into a relationship with them. If they are not quite right, I cannot take them in. Sometimes, a color will need another dip into another color to become the hue that is needed for the series. Recently, I completed a series on the Metals and created a set of silks for copper, silver, gold, bronze, tin, and other metals. I was having difficulty finding the color for Bronze. I would dye silks and it wouldn't be right. Then I dreamed the formula. Bronze came to me and told me which dyes to use to get the proper hue. The next day, I followed the instruction of my Bronze dream and there it was—B r o n z e.

I have an implicit trust in the form itself, that because of its purity it is able to hold whatever one can conceive of, whatever one is working with, if the intention is purely aligned. I have been able to dive deeper and deeper into my own spiritual questions, path, and guidance. I have been able to lead people into knowing and trusting the magnificence of who they are without imposing my own beliefs upon them. Layers and layers of peaks and valleys, like the Adirondack Mountains over Lake Champlain mark this rigorous and rewarding journey. This is what I hoped for: to help people, not as my followers, but to help them discover their own inner conversations, threads, paths, and teachers, and to trust their process enough to follow it. It is one of the greatest gifts I have been given in this life. To witness the spiritual development and trust and discovery of others, to witness their magnificence shining. It is an unspeakable gift.

The Silks

In the following pages lie the silks. Currently there are dozens and dozens of colors and some of them you see here. The colors are brought into or arise out of meditation for what is needed for the movement group or what color wants to be worked with on a universal level for the world and the prayers that are currently being called forward.

Then I create the silk, stirring, cooking, praying until the color feels just right. From there the silks and the colors that vibrate through them, facilitate, augment, carry, and move the prayers that are present in the hearts of those who work with them. Sometimes they serve a group, an individual, or sometimes nature herself.

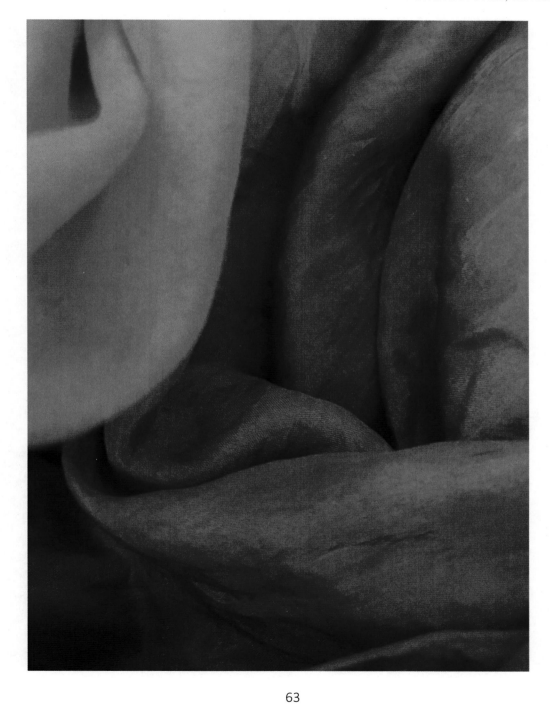

Embodied Prayer

Recently, the work has been directly with embodied prayer using the body as an intentional vehicle to pray. Letting the prayer be movement.

Prayer in movement is sometimes received. A person connects with the prayer as far as they know it. As they begin to move, they may notice that rather than moving the prayer outwardly, they are actually receiving something now from the prayer being in the heart or spoken and through movement. They are receiving a response. I have also found that at times after connecting fully, there is a sense of action in the body and through the body as though it is communicating, "This is what I must do." The movements then seem to be based on an active relationship within the prayer and the heavens.

A third observation I have recognized is that the mover becomes a channel of sorts. He or she allows something to come through them that is not necessarily personally relatable. This may be an angel, a guide, an aspect of nature, a time period, a nation, an individual, or an animal.

Offerings

In many cases I include and support and suggest making an offering in conjunction with Authentic Movement. This is part of placing the form in ceremony.

For each series I, either publicly with the knowledge and intention of the whole, or quietly, privately, internally, hold the group for the duration knowing that something larger is moving throughout the series.

For example, if we are doing a series on colors and working with the vibration of color each week, one can expect that there will be internal dimensions of color vibrations opening and unfolding over the course of the series in a big way. Depending upon the personal prayer or work of each individual, this will unfold differently. The movement filters out into life. Authentic Movement becomes authentic living, authentic life.

I ask people to begin to notice and carry forward the sense and energy of the inner witness moving out into life. Notice what is authentic in each moment. In any given day, in any given moment, what are you called to do? What is true here? Is there an action you are to embody? Is there a stillness or a listening that is yours to do? Are you to deeply witness something? A partner, a child, a grouping of trees, the movement of the clouds?

This is the prayer. In the studio, in the movement, in the body, in the circle, when we allow and invite our deepest self forward, there is a stepping up and an unpeeling both at once.

This is my prayer for the circle and it is also my prayer for all of humanity: at the pace that is correct for each individual, to ask for and invite cloudiness and shields to fall away, for falsities to fall away, to allow penetration or dissolving, so that the truer, more unguarded, immediate and more authentic self can emerge with room and permission to express. What is expressed at this time can be very personal. It can also be very connected to the cosmic or the collective. We all have guardians and beings and energies who work with us. Some people are aware of them, some people not. If we make an active invitation to an energy to be present and move with us, it is going to show up. And it is going to work with us to the depth that we allow it to. This can be a gentle process or a thunderous one. The circle holds it all.

To make an offering is to acknowledge this exchange, to acknowledge that in ceremony, we are in relationship. We are not alone, there is an exchange. Something is being given and we offer something as well. We are not in isolation, we are not really self-sustaining, we are sustained, and we are sustained in a force, an energy that is loving and is love.

Participants make offerings and prayers in many ways. Sometimes the offering is the simplicity of the breath and the prayer in the heart. Sometimes the offering is a song, sometimes a feather or a flower, a painting, a poem, a seed, a stone, a shell, a photograph, a perfume or essential oil, whatever is in the heart of the mover to offer or whatever presents itself as wanting to be offered.

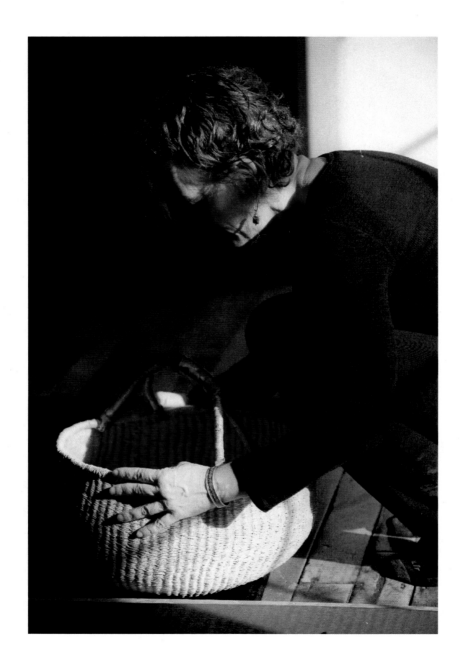

Objects

I invite people to select, find, create objects that help them to internally connect to their inner witness, whatever that is for them. This is never perfect as no object can represent that state; however, attempting to objectify the inner witness causes us to think and be with it in a very thoughtful way. In the choosing of an object, something may be learned by the mover about their inner witness. Then they know something more about their own essence. Does my inner witness feel to me like a clear ball, or a grove of trees, or the color blue, or an animal, like a big cat or an owl? What is the nature of the presence that witnesses your existence? Is it all loving? Is it personal or very aloof and impersonal? Does it call you by name? Do you feel an inner critic rather than an inner witness? If so, what is the inner critic like? Is it familiar? foreign? Is there something below or above that which is all accepting?

To find an object to represent this helps one to hold onto it, to examine it, to be with it, and as that inner sense of the witness changes, it becomes even more clear as the object that once felt so correct, now perhaps does not. The inner witness is actually un-nameable, indescribable. However, to approximate a quality of that presence invites an awareness of that energy to come into focus. Following is a fabricated example. A person might choose a stone as representative of their inner witness for a number of reasons. Perhaps the stone is from a time or place where they felt really in touch with their essence. Perhaps the stone feels grounding or solid and they feel deep comfort with the stone. Perhaps the stone communicates directly with them and through it, they feel very centered. Two years later, many changes have occurred and the quality of their inner witness now feels different. No longer a stone, now a bowl of clear water exemplifies more closely the inner presence that sees and holds without judgment. One is not better than the other, but something inwardly has shifted, and is demonstrated in the choice of object.

Tracking

In Authentic Movement, there is a practice that Janet Adler called tracking. To track is to stay with awareness of everything that is occurring for you and around you, whether you are the mover or the witness. For example, if you are a mover, and like the mover in the photo below who frequently moves with an intricate highly charged movement of her hands and fingers and

breath which then activates something in the wholeness of her body, to track this would be to witness inwardly and to remember as fully as possible, " What is my journey."

"I lift my left hand overhead, the energy is pulling me upward. As I lift my hand, my ribcage opens up and I am aware of a space inside of me. It is hot there and I can hear an inner sound. The color is orange, like there is a great orange heat in my ribs, heart, lungs. I begin to blow and make sounds. This feels good and is releasing the heat inside The blowing gets stronger and stronger as my hands take on quick and changing gestures. They are too fast to track, I feel moved by something much bigger than me and that my job is to simply stay with it."

This is a fabricated but plausible example of someone tracking their inner experience. When one tracks, several things stand out. You learn whether your predominant modes of access are the sensations of your body, the emotions, how the body is in space, the images that arise, or numerous other modes of perception and connection unique to each individual. This is helpful for several reasons. As a mover, when you are in a place of stasis, you can bring awareness to the predominant mode you are in and change it. For example, if you find yourself returning again and again to a pattern of moving with sadness or regret or anger or an old belief like, "I am always left out," if you know inwardly that you are in a closed circle, that you have been here a hundred times before and there is no way out through the emotional body, you can bring your attention away from the emotion to the sensations in your body, "I am so hot," or "I am so heavy and weighted," and begin to move the heat, or move from the deeply weighted place. Embody that. Or what is the image that arises from this cycle of sadness or anger? "I have the image of a caged tiger in me," or "the image of a three year old child lost in the woods" or of "a village burning to the ground." Then move from the emotional place to the imaginal world. Let the images dictate and lead your movements. You will break out of the cycle. Something new will be introduced.

Also through this practice you are keeping track of your holy path. You are coming to know the movements that are deeply connected to the holy for you, the movements that take you deeper into inner discovery, the inner conversation, the well-being, the flow. You begin to know your own doorways. Sometimes going through these doorways can take you to highly altered states. States where the ego is long gone and the sense of what it is to be *You* is also far, far away. Your boundaries are quite thin and you are accessing flows of energy from other realms or from so deep within the wise chasms of your body that there can be a strong sense of the non-human consciousness, cosmic consciousness, nature consciousness, the un-nameable. If you have been tracking and have developed the skill and practice of staying aware, your inner witness is with you, holding space, remembering center, preventing you from being consumed or lost in these states, remembering that you are riding some unfamiliar territory but because you are tracking, you have your path home. Eventually, the conscious practice of tracking becomes integrated. Tracking is no longer a separate thing that must be attended to but is seamless with the practice of Authentic Movement and carrying forward into the authenticity of Life itself.

This tracking practice extends to the witness as well. As you are witness, you may attend to what is happening internally for you, both as information for yourself and as information for your mover. For often the witness, when very open and clear will feel resonances in their own body that are in direct clear relationship to the mover. To offer those later in language can be very helpful to the mover. It can be a continuation through language of the movement itself.

Projections

I enter the movement space. Several people are already there. They are seated and talking, laughing, seemingly comfortable and light with each other. It is two minutes past the starting time. I am a bit later. There is one more person expected, we are waiting for her. This could be an example of a mover's inner experience, "I feel harsh and critical of these people, their laughter, their joviality. I feel critical of the facilitator that we are not beginning yet. I will walk to the other side of the room and physically separate myself."

The movement circle begins and then what could have solidified as a projection, because it is in the process of being owned, can instead move as follows: "As we begin, I tune in to myself, into the tightness, the tension brought on by the critical judgement I feel. I allow it, I move with it, it opens, more emotions come, I let them flow. Soon I am beyond emotion and simply in my body, deeper and deeper into my flow, my truth my sensations. Allowing has taken over and I am immersed in a kind of bliss."

This can happen with any feeling if it is owned. The feeling can transform and move. All feelings are based in movement. Emotions are full of motion. They are not set in stone or designed to hang around. They are moving information, moving expressions of the heart. Thoughts are the same. They move; they have shape and resonance and vibration and energy. When you think a thought, "I like this, I like her hair, I don't like that shirt. He is too tall, scruffy, withheld, loud," its energy can be felt. It has an impression. When you own that thought or that feeling and recognize that it is something that is living in you, it is then something that you can move, something that can open to its fuller roots, something that can reveal a depth in you that you formerly perhaps did not know. It can bring you closer toward your essence by dismantling or dissolving an edge, a weapon. Being energy and movement, the body is a perfect vehicle for unwinding, unraveling this energy, pure and direct.

If the thought or emotion is not owned, but is instead projected out onto the group or onto a certain person—"That person is ridiculous, dangerous, too loud, too quiet," "This group is doing it wrong, will never meet my needs, doesn't understand who I am,"—then the unowned energy becomes a projected thought form in the group space, unowned and rather unlovable for the most part. It can feel like a fog, a pall, a density, a curtain, a stone in the group. A subduing of the whole. It is now a weapon that is present in the circle and the effect it has on others is that they feel it and depending upon their ability to stand with unknown weapons, they may or may not feel safe enough to move freely with their own inner dynamics.

When we don't own what is ours, it affects the whole. What we don't own is not a secret. It is felt and perceived by the whole. It is simply not named.

Then, because Authentic Movement is the movement energy form that it is, someone who is open and able may encounter the thought form or the projected emotion in the space and move it through their own body. They may or may not know, this is mine or this is not mine but I am moving it anyway. Because we are working in an open field, this can and does happen. And the originator of the emotion may feel better or they could still be generating more of the same thought form or projected emotion. Some may be unharmed by the weapon. But some who may be more fragile, could be affected by the weapon in some way that hopefully will be meaningful for them and healing for them. However, if the originator of the thought or feeling does not own the projection, it is not rendered whole within themselves.

The Signature

For each person, the experience of being at their center is different. How they arrive there is also a unique journey. What is the road for each mover?

One cannot will oneself into a spiritual flowing grace-filled center. One cannot intend it in that way. We can listen more deeply, feel more deeply, trust more fully, open more fully, soften more completely. As we practice these things, there is a natural surrender that happens. This surrendering will happen through the physical, psychological, historical, spiritual channels of who we are and how we are formed as a human being. Each person discovers this on their own through the practice of Authentic Movement, through trusting, listening, and allowing movement. The movements themselves hold the meaning and significance that is behind the ego structure. Through surrendering, the ego slightly dissolves or perhaps, rests quietly so that the larger or more essential authentic self can have space to manifest.

One person may travel down a road of very deep emotion to access this place, experiencing tremendous grief, their own grief, past their own grief into world grief, opening their hearts and bodies to feel and express and trust that they are okay and they can go down this well. Then at some point, it is possible that something will shift.

Personally, I am a grief traveler. I learn many things through the openheartedness and surrender of grief. When I feel grief, I take it seriously as a sign from the heavens to follow it down. I have followed grief so completely down and down and down into a well, past personal grief into collective grief into universal grief.

I will recount one particular movement experience. It begins with a feeling of grief around the death of my brother. I move with this. As I move with it, I am drawn down into the purity of grief. It is no longer *about my brother,* but simply grief itself. I keep allowing the feeling, traveling down. Now, I travel so far down into the grief space, nothing else exists. There are no landmarks. I am on the ground in a sobbing heap. I know I am at the bottom of what feels like all the grief that ever was. Even though there are 20 people in the room with me, I feel singular and very distant from them, removed from their world. This is not frightening at all, it simply is.

Now I hear and feel a presence inside of me say to me clearly "Get up. Stand Up. You cannot stay down. Stand up." I follow the order. I stand. When I stand, the Silence I perceive is pure holiness. I stand in palpable Silence. Out of the Silence emerges the most exquisite sound I have ever heard, the harmony of the spheres. It is the voice of the angels singing. I look, with my eyes closed, to the east and see a very bright light and a grove of trees far off in the distance. The sound continues. "What is this?" I ask inwardly. "This is the place where angels are born," is what I am told. Oh, on all levels of body, mind and spirit, I am in a profound state of oneness, radiance, and grace, timeless. I am forever changed.

That was one journey through grief to profound grace and holiness. Did I know that would happen? No, absolutely not. I simply knew and know that grief is one of my doorways to the holy. For me, grief is so full of helpers, angels, spiritual assistance, there is no fear as long as I keep surrendering.

For another person, their road or one of their roads might be to travel into the folds in their body, very sensual looking, fluid, wavy dissolving movements, going deeper and deeper into that, trusting, surrendering, entering. After a while they may notice that their thoughts have stopped, their emotions are very quiet and they are pure movement, primal waves, and profound inner peace.

For another person, it is necessary for them to fall into abandon with their voice, to use sound to surrender into, deeper and deeper explorations of surrender into sound which can open into an experience of channeling certain sounds that are both personal and necessary for the group to hear and work with or for the world to hear and work with. Or a song may come through completely formed that the mover has never heard before. It sings itself. Strange sounds may emerge from the mover. Again, it is the act of surrendering to how the body is moving, perceiving, feeling. The *you* follows rather than leads.

Still another person may enter this state of surrender through contact with another mover, the interplay, the exchange, the give and take, you and I merging. Another person may know that when they slow their movements way down, their awareness intensifies. They are able to become more present in their movements and thus their body, heart, mind, and spirit.

One's deep pathway cannot be taught. It must be uncovered. It must be unfolded, discovered. It comes from within. It is crucial that it be allowed unconditionally by the witness and it must be allowed also by the mover. If you are the mover, you are the one who must allow your own deep unfolding. To do that, trust is essential. Trust in the witness, and trust, primarily in yourself. You are the one feeling the feelings and sensations, hearing the sounds, both inner and outer, having the visions and the impulses. You are the one being directed from inside. It is not taught, but uncovered, developed, and allowed.

Northeast Kingdom

The colors. As a child, my path was already formed. I believe I entered with it singing its song. It demanded of me, led me, beckoned me to go outside the lines. To find the edges. To cross over, to listen to small and unintelligible voices and to listen deeply to these as though everything depended upon deciphering the undecipherable, the language that has no words. I was born feeling everything, born into vibration, born revering and answering to color, to sound, to energy, to the unseen and un-nameable. I was born knowing God and knowing the mystery of life as my primary relationship, my primary teacher. I was born trusting what I could not describe. I did not understand why others around me did not and why no one spoke of what was completely obvious: that we are held, that love is everywhere. I recall seeing and feeling the huge pain bodies in my family operating, running the show, drawing the consciousness of the family always toward the pain, toward a kind of hopelessness and underlying acceptance that this is what we have. It felt similar to a train on a train track moving to only one destination when we had a huge open field all around us that we could easily be exploring. We could simply step off the track and be in this field. It's right there. I was astounded that there was no hope or idea that it could be any other way, but instead a continual acceptance of what was unacceptable. This would be punctuated by moments of beauty, deep caring, deep love and yet the baseline was always this pain that we must begin from, day after day after day. It seemed centered around my father and what appeared on the surface to be a lack of fulfillment, a profound lack of self-esteem, as though he was chained to the family by cement blocks. When really it seemed as though he wanted not something from or for this future but something from his past that was undone, unfinished, unrealized, as though his path should have gone in a different direction and now he had no idea how to live the life he had landed in. Alcohol numbed it, heightened it, aggravated it, soothed it, occupied his attention to distract him from it.

I am one self who occupies many different realities, many different perspectives. As a child I prayed for my father, I prayed for my mother as well but she seemed more cared for somehow, more self-sustained. My father seemed intolerably sad and his sadness and unhappiness directed the movement or non-movement of the family.

At night, I would pray fervently for my family that they would stay together, that my father's pain would be healed, that he would find a way to fulfillment and beyond his sadness. Although my mother taught me certain prayers as a child and she would come into my room each night to hear my prayers and I would say them in front of her with her as the witness, it would really only be after she left my room that the real prayers began. That I would open my heart and open a space to really speak with God. I would speak about the nature of the struggle, I would speak of my worry for the family. I did not understand how we could exist as a cohesive whole and I did not understand how we could not. I could always feel the ripping away at the seams, the shredded way the family felt held together and that it always seemed to be just by the sheer will of my mother that we remained together. My father, in spite of pleading and cajoling and threatening and reasoning and loving, did not change.

I wondered then how God answered prayers. Were my prayers being answered, being heard? They were answered in the day by dailyness of life continuing on. They were answered by the fact that my mother never did leave my father. They were answered by year after year of Thanksgiving dinners and birthdays and Christmas celebrated. They were answered by those moments of complete love and joy and respect and caring that rose out of the sea of sadness like great sperm whales, breaking the surface, uplifting the heart, a break in the clouds when the crystalline blue of the sky can be seen. And somehow that would be enough. That would be what I would get and that would be enough to know that yes, my prayers are heard. I am not alone. I am not without my circle of holiness, without my circle of source, without my circle of origin.

As a very young child, my family lived in the old Victorian house of my grandmother. On the landing going from the first to the second floor, there was a window seat with a burgundy tufted cushion and a stained glass window. The window had colors of deep ruby red, blues in different shades, clear, yellow-gold and green. I would sit there at two years old, three years old, four years old with the colors, with the glass. I would touch the colors with my fingers and mingle with them. I would experience being immersed in the singularity of each color, that the air around me for example was ruby red. I was in red, breathing red, feeling red on my skin, among red, inside of red. I would do the same with each color as I touched it. I would enter it. I was in a complete ecstasy there on the window seat with the colors, and with the vibration that they are. Something true in my soul was awakened and recognized through the interaction with the colors and their interaction with me. Did my mother or father or anybody know about this? No, I am sure they did not. It was a private and deep reverie, to speak of it would have diminished it to a statement about my vivid imagination rather than the exquisitely real experience that it was.

I felt the presence of Colors as a guardian or a sister. Now decades later, I bring back the relationship with color to the form of Authentic Movement, to the form of moving prayer.

Transition

I open myself in prayer to what the next series is to be about. Sometimes the colors come first, sometimes the intention comes first and the colors follow. Once the colors come, they will often come to me in a dream or a meditation as the vibration that they are. I see them inwardly and then I work toward creating them in real form in the silks. Sometimes they will tell me that they want to work in a group, that they have a specific job to do. They tell me through a wordless image, vibration, or knowing. I rarely hear them speak in words, but I do hear their sound.

It is as though the colors know what I am doing, they want to help, they want to participate and in fact, sometimes they lead the show. I know that as a silk is created and the color is introduced, it will extend its vibration into all the levels of prayer and consciousness that are accessed and generated. It will work with the whole group, it will work with individuals, it will work with a broader consciousness. I experienced the seed of this as a child and I have a certain authority or relationship with it. The authority comes through opening so deeply to the colors and the deep knowing that arises from that. It is not an idea. I love the colors as I know the relationship to God that they are. I know the sound they make in the other dimensions.

A number of months ago, the group was working with several silks that were very pale blue and several pale pinks, off white and what I call Evergreen Breath. Deep into the series, I realized that the colors were a discipline. They were holding the movers to a limited palette, to deep inner energy, to not extending outwardly, in order to deepen the practice of prayer, trusting deeply inwardly, turning to one's own center rather than outside of oneself and listening to subtleties and what is hidden in the quiet.

Prayer

It snows now lightly here in the Northeast Kingdom. My dog is by my side. As I begin writing this piece, she lifts her head, listening. She knows what we are doing, she knows why we are here. She is patient and attentive. She is listening into the deep outdoors. We have set up a medicine wheel, it is out there working on our behalf. She is paying attention. She hears, sees, smells, senses the animals of the forest. Yesterday, she was the outsider, today she has established her presence. She belongs now. She is tracking who comes here, where and when. She is spreading her own scent, finding her place. She cannot find her place if she does not spread her scent. If she does not reveal herself and make her presence known she will not find her place, she will remain the outsider, the one who does not belong.

There is a vulnerability in marking one's place, in letting one's presence be known, be seen, heard, felt, witnessed. You render yourself visible, you render a stand you are taking. The vulnerability comes in as we live in a world rife with duality, a world that could easily try to find fault, to take an oppositional stand, to use what you stand for as a weapon, as a point of contention. Then what? Do you defend?

This is the work. This is where the prayers land and the work lands. This is where my interest and work is. It goes all the way back to when I was born. I was looking for the way beyond the conflict, beyond the weaponry, beyond the wars.

As a child and as a young woman in my 20's, I dreamt of war often. War-torn countries. War-torn battlegrounds. In my dreams, it seemed like the war was freshly over or perhaps between battles and I was walking through the rubble with my grandmother. There were wounded everywhere, destruction was everywhere. We were walking through, walking through. In many ways, living has been like this. Along with the beauty, the war-torn must be seen, must be included.

How do we go beyond the place of weaponry and duality? This is my focus in the work. To take a stand in one's deepest place of center and connection is to take a stand in the living stream of the divine. Here one is immersed in the place of essence, inseparable from one's own.

This is a unique place. No one else can claim it, for it belongs only to the one whose vibration resonates with it. There is only one. There can be no argument with it as the vibration is with the wholeness, the flow, the ecstatic state. The practice is to stay with the higher vibration, to allow the oneness, and to allow the energy to flow.

This is easier said than done, for as we do this, we face the feeling of dissolving, of losing our identity. The grip of our ego and self-reflection takes a back seat to how the divine sees, knows, and moves us. When we are here in this essence, standing, taking a stand, moving, witnessing, acting, the flow is supporting us. However, the action is never fully about us. We step out of the way at the same time we must fully show up. We fully show up as an instrument of divine will and yet our free will is essential as an engaged element. We yoke to the bigger picture, we trust the bigger picture, we feel the energy behind it, we allow it, we open our bodies, we step out of the way and allow ourselves to be moved. We trust that what comes forward, although it may be unfamiliar to our egos, is coming from the body and the body's wisdom as a vehicle for consciousness.

Practicing this in the studio through the form of Authentic Movement gives way to allowing yourself to live life in this way, to live every moment in this way and to allow your life to become a holy practice.

You are not dying, but you are dissolving. The dissolution is both the heaviness, the armor, the debris giving itself up as a shield and the entry, the flow of your natural divine essence. It feels like dissolving or dying because you are literally becoming lighter—less dense, less compacted, less contracted. There is less effort required for living and moving. There is more going with the flow. It may be more possible to feel the universe answering you back.

The prayers are jewels of focus. The prayers are linked to the deep heart of the movers. When I call the movers to pray, they go to a place in their Inner Being spirit that means business. They go to the place where they are struggling or grappling with something, where their heart is alive, pumping, caring, loving. They go to the place where things really matter to them, to the place where their energy or essence is alive. This place may be personal or collective. It does not matter. What matters is the quality of presence that is evoked, the quality of alignment. We all move through places where we are in prayer for our own personal benefit or salvation of the soul and places where we are praying on behalf of others or praying for the world's consciousness to move in a certain direction.

If we are in touch with the aliveness of the cells of our bodies, the holiness of the breath of life, the *evergreen breath*, we are in touch with essence. When we set our focus in line with what truly matters in our hearts and souls, we invoke an energy that is yoked to divine energy.

We are now in a state of holy reception. All the cells of our bodies are like a tuning fork. We are primed for listening and our bodies are an openly receptive vehicle for moving. Our ego is quiet, having given over our free will and our ego's will to be in partnership with the energy of the larger will that is speaking to us. As it is speaking to us through the vehicle of the body, it is here that we listen.

Listening to our sensations, listening to the urges of the body, reading the landscape of our own interiority and riding the edge, bringing the urges forward, without ever knowing in what direction they will go, what the outcome will be, we are receiving. Is there a tightness in the belly, a feeling of lightness, or flight in the arms? Does the body want to fly? Is there a vision, a cave to enter, a desert to traverse, a being to encounter? Is there a sound pushing its way to the surface? We allow the body to move and be formed, to sound, to touch, to connect, to emote, to go deep and deep and deeper still into the potency that is there. We are the followers, our movements are the painting, we are painting it but we know not what we paint. What is happening? Is this my prayer being asked? Is this the answer being given? Is this answer for me? For someone else, For the collective?

We are in a collective field of oneness. There are permeable boundaries around the idea of self. We are in a field of prayer. Everyone's prayer is moving here. One may be actually working with something for someone else and they may be working with something for another. The intention and prayer of one has now merged and melded with the intention and prayer of another with whom there was a resonance. The mystery begins, the mystery acts, the synchronicities happen, the harmonies happen. The embodiment occurs.

There is something very special about the embodiment of the prayers, the movement of the prayers and the witnessing of these prayers. Because the embodiment is, of course, on the physical level and the consciousness is as awake and aware as possible, there is a clarity and lightness of flow of energy in the body. The prayers get moved on a physical level and are then entered into the world as being *Born*. The prayers are *Born*.

I am certain that it has always been so to one degree or another, but the time we live in is now and the effect that we can have is now. The times are critical, in a day by day and moment by moment balance. The practice of Authentic Movement with the sense of the eyes of the heart open allows the movers to connect intentionally with the bigger picture of focus and intention for bringing things into balance on a broader scale.

Living Authentically

I return now to the dream I had many years ago which I spoke of earlier. In that dream, I am moving in a movement circle and I am given clear direction to open my eyes. Opening the eyes is not something that happens in Authentic Movement normally, as to open one's eyes means you are moving from the place of the deep inner world to the place of wide awake conscious day world. The dream, I believe, was showing me, demanding of me, the necessity to do both, to be in touch with the deep wisdom that comes uniquely and singularly to each of us while at the same time living with eyes wide open, witnessing the world, bringing to the world the same level of deep attention to what is happening in the world, knowing that this deep attention energetically changes the direction of the flow.

How does one act? How does one discern what is the correct action to take? When is it my turn to not simply witness but to step in? To trust that action. That this action belongs to me, it is mine to do. If I do not do it, the moment passes by. The action remains undone. If the urge is there and I am in alignment with that urge, I am backed by Creation.

Here is a fictitious example. Imagine you are in a public space. You see one person being harmed by another. Politeness would have it that we turn away, depending upon the level of harm, that we mind our own business. Let's say that there is an urging in us to not turn away. There is an action that belongs to us to do. If we turn away, we will be left empty, unfinished or unfulfilled. If we turn away, we will not allow the energy to shift through us. If we turn away, the other people involved do not benefit from our attention to the situation.

Perhaps we hesitate because we do not know how to intervene without becoming part of the problem. The question and the answer are one and the answer will lie in the moment itself. Perhaps, you are to speak or act directly. Perhaps you are to introduce kindness, perhaps you are simply to witness, to not turn away. Perhaps the situation is dangerous and you are to turn to an intricate solution. The point is, you are being called to take action, to grapple with the situation. We have authority as human beings to act in accordance with human ethics. When we see harm being done, it is correct that we respond, whether that response is an inner one of witnessing or an outer one of right action.

Here is an illustration. In the movement circle, one mover is moved to very deep emotion. She is crying audibly and deeply as she stands wrapped in a reddish purple silk that she has found with her eyes closed. Does she know its color? I do not know. I stand a witness. Another mover feels an inner call to go to her. She stands behind her. She does not attempt to stop the crying but is supporting the crying mover. We do not know what the mover is crying about. Is it personal? Is it collective? Is it universal? Is it her emotion or is she expressing something for the group or for another mover? Does she know? Does she not know? She knows - I am the one who is sad, who has tears to cry. I feel the tears, I let them flow, I express what is moving through my body. The mover who stands behind simply knows—I am to be with this crying mover. I am to be with the sadness that is being expressed. My body calls me here. I am to stand behind her. A third mover hears an inner call. She herself is placed at the center of the room, at the post that has come to symbolically be the Tree of Life. In her hands is a Violet silk. Does she know it is Violet? Perhaps yes, perhaps no. What she knows is that the vibration of the silk in her hand is to go to that crying mover. That she knows. And that she does. She crawls, holding the silk, to the one who cries. Does she know someone is already there? It doesn't matter. She knows that it is her place to go and that it is important that she bring what she brings. The silk is long, and as it happens, it stays in alignment with the center post, to the Tree of Life, at the same time that it is reaching toward the crying mover. This second mover comes in front of the crying mover and stays on her knees. Now the crying mover is surrounded, sandwiched in between two energetic loving bodies.

Her crying subsides after a while. The three movers stay together for a long time. I am witnessing this. The feeling that rises in me is profound love and caring moving through all three movers. They have become one. They have merged energetically into one flow of love. The love unites them and dissolves their boundaries. In those moments, they are immersed in a unified field.

Had the crying mover said, "I cannot cry, I must hold this back," none of this would have happened. Had the mover who came from behind not listened to that urge to come and stand behind, her strong loving energy would not have been present. The crying mover would not have felt the backing, so that when the third mover came with the silk, it would have been a very different experience. Had the third mover with the silk not come or not brought the silk, she would possibly have been concerned with the fact that she was to bring something but did not and her attention would be divided, not fully with the crying mover, and so there would be an incompleteness about her gesture, her attention not fully engaged. Had she not come, would someone else have come? Would the crying mover's front stay open and empty? She, the third mover, had she not followed her urge, may have gone on in her movement, with something vaguely or acutely discomforting. Perhaps it would have brought her into another important movement of her own. Into her own emotion.

At the same time this was going on, there were several other movers who heard the crying, were aware of the crying and were not called to go to that mover. They were engaged in their own energetic flow that did not call them to this mover. That was not their work. It was not theirs to do. It was not where they belonged. They could have gone out of a sense of guilt or duty, a socialized dictate that says we must always help, we must always comfort, we must always be there. Rather than listening to the deeper call of their own bodies, they may have gone and their sense of ambivalence may have been perceived by the crying mover. They perhaps would have been rejected by her or, the movement of love that occurred would not have happened and the energy bodies would not have been open to receive it.

It is possible the energy that the other movers were engaged in was related to the crying mover, but in a different way, a different aspect of the whole. They were needed to be doing exactly what they were doing for the whole of the energetic body to be realized. "While you cry, I cover my head and my eyes. I go deeper into the darkness. May this assist you on your journey into the pain. May my action give you courage to go deeper." Or conversely, the mover who cries expresses the grief that the others feel but do not express.

Regarding vulnerability, I was speaking earlier about how sometimes people stay closed because it can be frightening to be in that unknown place of flow. We can see it clearly here with these three movers in an embrace of complete unified energy. They are embracing; all three are giving and receiving all at once. Who is the giver and who is the receiver? There is little ego in control, what is happening then? They are in a merged state of unified field of oneness expressing love. To whom? To each other? To the group? To the world? For the world? Who and what is receiving this profound expression as it vibrates out? They are creating and manifesting and moving an expression of love and unified oneness that is going out into humanity. As an example, as a gift, perhaps it will be perceived across the country or across the ocean by someone who needs to know that this is possible, perhaps it will be perceived by a family member or by another mover in the room. They have created the vibration, the resonance, and it is free to resonate out. Standing in one's place of belonging has profound implications.

This mover wraps her head, wraps her already closed eyes. Another mover wraps her head, wraps her already closed eyes. They are not aware on a conscious level that the other has done this as well. On an inner level perhaps something knows, for now in the synchronicity of the circle the two wrapped head movers find each other and begin a movement together. The meaning of it will never be adequately named, but the grace of it is apparent, is clear. They are each doing what they know is theirs to do in the moment, aware, not of the specificity of the synchronicity, but feeling the flow of its existence. They are running on an inner fire that keeps them moving steadily.

104

In the outer world, the day world, the wide wake world, how does this relate? How do we stay awake and alive and true? How do we stay with the kernel of what matters, what is in our hearts, when so much pulls us to do otherwise. I know of the divinity of life. I am also a firm advocate of freedom and the openness of form. I am fascinated by forms, by structures, by the things people create or discover to help them to understand their lives, their world. I study these in fascination. I use them, I incorporate them. But I do not believe in them as absolutes. I have developed trust over the years in my own inner knowing, which I distinguish from belief. The inner knowing is settled and unshakable, like the sky that is always there, day or night. One can always look to the sky. Believing feels more like a direction, an arrow, a guidepost. For me, the two of them, knowing and believing, work together. The beliefs remain somewhat fluid and changeable as new knowing is revealed.

Together, they can form an intrinsic map or container for one's life. This will be unique for each person, intrinsic guidelines and boundaries to guide one towards the deepest, truest place in oneself. That deepest truest place has its own energy and pull that is always drawing one towards it. I marvel at the human being, at the incredibly creative creations that we are. My heart yearns for each of us to fully realize who we are and what we are capable of.

When I look out at nature, I am immersed in beauty. The beauty stands. The beauty is. The beauty emanates. The beauty graces. The beauty resonates and connects and holds the world. The beauty sings. When I look out at human beings, I see beauty hidden, beauty shy, beauty hurt, beauty strangled, beauty blocked, beauty frightened, beauty angry, as well as beauty flowing, beauty trying, beauty inspired, beauty singing, beauty creating, beauty being.

As humans, we are complicated. The path is not an easy one for anyone. We have been given the blessing and the responsibility of free will. We have choice in every moment. We can chose a path that opens and clarifies or we can choose a path that causes us and others pain. The pain belongs to all of us. The grace and flow and song also belong to all of us. Sitting here and writing this book, part of me wants to stop. Wants to get up and go outside, wants to walk my dog in the park, to do what I am accustomed to. But instead, I have come here to the woods. I know that it is time. I know that if I don't do it now, I won't do it. How do I know that? I just know it. It is a knowing revealed to me that it is time. I brought a marble candle holder from Italy that was given to me by a dear friend in Bellagio, a place where I spoke of beginning this book. I light the candle here when I write. I resist lighting it because it means I am going to actually write. I resist what I know I must do when the doing is hard. It is not easy to apply oneself. But there is flow, there is support, as I accomplish something that comes from the knowing, something that is mine to do.

I notice that there is something about accomplishment that can be difficult for humanity. It means going somewhere new, breaking out of comfort and repetition. It means being awake and applying oneself. It means trusting that it matters even if it is hard. Even if no one is watching and no one is approving or disapproving, can you still do it? Because it is yours to do, you are the one who is being urged from inside. It is that inside place that urges that I call God speaking, destiny calling. I don't know what you are urged to do, but I support it if it is in alignment with creation and a sense of the inherent beauty that runs and organizes this world. Beauty outweighs destruction. Beauty realizes. Beauty rises. Beauty uplifts. Destruction sinks and takes down, but ultimately makes way for more beauty.

If we, as a species were to actually destroy this earth, which we are capable of, we would destroy ourselves. The earth would prevail. Time would be irrelevant, life would return. That would be a tragedy of tremendous proportions because the human race, the human species is capable of so much creative goodness. The creativity is happening all the time, everywhere. We can't help it. We do it, we are made for it. But it is as though somehow people feel that their authority to act in this manner has been diminished. As though we need permission. There have been and are places and times when outer authorities throughout the ages have overpowered and hence squelched, frightened, harmed. This remains with us as collective memory. But we have everything we need now to go beyond this. These memories of difficult times are just that, memories, truths that happened in the past. We do not need to be ruled by what is over.

It doesn't matter to me in what way you are inspired in the divine flow, but it does matter to me that you are inspired, that we as a collective are inspired and that humanity as a whole realizes itself. That matters to me. Very deeply. I work with it continuously in small ways, in bigger ways, in really big ways.

I try to help people to remember who they are, to honor who they are and to find ways to live as who they are in God, whatever that means to them, whatever they name that essence: Creation, Oneness, Essence, Divinity, the All, Nature, Center, Heart. This matters so much to me. Perhaps it goes back to my father and my brother, whose lives were both beautiful and tragic. I learned through them an important lesson of authentic living. I learned that their pain was not more important than my life, than my inspiration, than my connection with God. I learned through being in touch with my inner being that as they were the crying movers, the angry movers, the depressed movers, it was not my job, my place, my movement to be the one picking them up in the intimate way. It was not my responsibility to try to heal them, but rather to witness and hold their journeys with understanding and compassion. This was incredibly painful to stay with and to trust.

I knew and felt that their pain was magnetic, was unsolvable by me and even unsolvable by them. I knew that they would not get out of this particular life beyond their own pain. And I knew that were I to give too much of my energy and focus and life force to them, I would go down into their abyss. I could feel it. I could feel the abyss, its pull, its power and how somehow, they were comfortable though miserable in it. This was not for me. My life had another direction and was not to be sacrificed. The pain of this truth was and remains a great lesson. I have no regrets, and yet am witness to their pain and to my own.

Through this, I learned the great lesson of acceptance. To be able to accept what cannot be changed, to step away, to refocus, to put energy where it moves and flows, to love someone as they are, to witness them even when they are in a deep stasis. I know that the energy of witnessing creates a space that allows and facilitates change. It is not mine to determine timing. I am an instrument of God. I cannot say when. I can listen to when. I can listen to time and space interacting and feel the energy and step into action at the right time. But I do not control time. I am here in the grace of time, for as long as I am given, before I return to the eternal state in all ways. I take all of this seriously. Every day, every moment. I do not forget what I am doing.

Authentic living is a name I am using for the purposes of illustration, of explanation, to encourage people, those I know and those I don't know, to live from the deep true place. Authentic living is a not a coined term, it isn't a method, it is completely natural, it is within each of us already. It is a prayer and a hope of remembrance. To trust yourself and that you are composed of goodness. That beauty is a way of life. That holiness and beauty are one. Beauty's signature is a sign that you are on the right path. It is a moment by moment journey. But you can, as my friend says, "Set a course." You have the authority to set the course in your life. Examples could be, I am setting the course to paint 12 paintings this year and have them in galleries on every continent. I am setting the course to open the communication with my husband, my wife, my daughter, my son this year. I am setting the course to broaden my effect in the global warming scene this year. I am setting the course to be in better relationship with my body this year. I am setting the course to teach 10 workshops this year. I am setting the course to plant a garden this year.

Set your course. Grapple with what arises if it is yours to do. Remember that the question and the answer are linked, are one. Be with the flow. It doesn't mean that it will be easy, or what you want, but it will be flowing.

Sometimes people become confused when something is not exactly what they wanted. The ego tends to want things to be a certain way. We don't often get that. That does not mean that you are not on your path or that you are being punished. It means that in the flow of life, you are in a co-creative dynamic. There is universal will and there is personal will. The confluence of the two is where the flow happens. The personal will alone can cause tremendous havoc. The listening and discernment and alignment with the holy nature of life brings about co-creation. I follow that. Sometimes I will like it, sometimes not. But I will feel that it is right. Through it, I will feel that I belong there, even if I don't *like* it. Even if it does not make me happy. I feel this is where I belong and if I move from this spot I will lose one of my threads. This is the thread for me to hold. This is mine to do. Perhaps, I am the one who stands at the wall, tracing with my hand, one hand lifted, fingers pointed, mouth pursed, making small sounds.

Do I like this? Do I not like it? This is irrelevant. What is relevant is that this is mine to do in this moment. I don't understand it with my conscious everyday mind, but I understand it with the deep flow that places me here in this time and space at this wall doing exactly this. I can do nothing else. I belong here. And because I am here doing this, so much else that I have no control over or knowledge of can happen. I am in the web, in the fabric, holding my thread and the garment of humanity is being woven. It is humbling and exalted. What could be better than this?

Beginnings

We are given a life. We are given a starting point. We are given parents, a place of birth, we are given a body, we are given circumstances. Perhaps we choose all of this depending upon the work we are here to do. I believe we do, in co-creation. But whether we do or we do not, we are born into something.

In an Authentic Movement circle, we never know what will happen, just as in a life, we never know what will happen. Time after time it is unpredictable. Every circle is a mystery to be traversed, to be listened to, to be grappled with, to humbled by, to be exalted by, to reach into your truth with.

The bell rings, the movers close their eyes. As a mover, you leave the visible connection of the whole, the unified oneness, where each witness spreads her arms, where eye contact has circled around to each one. With eyes closed now, it is as though you have traveled the birth canal and are born into your separateness. You are suddenly in your interiority. You are with yourself, your existential aloneness. You are born. Who are you in this born self? What do you feel? What do you sense? What urges are calling to you? Where are you inspired or called or led? Can you remember the oneness you came from? What is your thread? You find your thread, you catch it, you hold it, you work with it, you are deeply connected to your thread; it feels right. You have had to trust deeply to find this, to trust what cannot be seen or named. You know where you belong. There is a feeling of *rightness, correctness* in you. Not necessarily happiness, but *rightness* as though something urges, I must do this. This can be as simple as lying face down on the floor, as still as fallen snow, or it can be endlessly complex, moving, dancing, sounding, interacting, making rhythm, standing upside down, rolling, spinning. The feeling of *rightness* is important. It is connected to the ability to discern. The development of discernment is essential for living a life that is fulfilled, not *happy* but fulfilled, on the path.

Here you are in the circle with your thread connected, moving, in your groove. Along comes another mover, whose eyes are also closed, who does not know that they will encounter you. They are in their groove, they are with their thread. What happens in that interaction is critical. This is where in life we often get tripped up. The other mover probably did not consciously choose to find you. How each of you was moving brought you together. Is it random? Is it meaningful? Is there something that the two of you are to do together?

Are you to co-create? Are you to expand your boundary now to include the energy of this other mover? If you do, can you do it without giving up your primary thread? Can you allow your thread to be influenced, perhaps transformed by the interaction with this other mover, over whom you have no control? Can you stay with yourself and why you were born while allowing life to affect you, blend with you? Can it be a joining rather than an opposition? Can it be a celebration rather than a war? Can you remember the place in God that you came from? Did God or Creation or Fate bring this mover to you as a gift? Or not? How do you discern? "Where and with what do I belong?" Sometimes saying No is as important as saying Yes.

In these photos, we see there is a mover with a wrapped head. She has been approached by, or encountered by another mover with a Violet silk. What happened when they met? I, as witness, see that the mover with the Violet silk took an action to wrap the shrouded head mover around her shoulders with the Violet silk. She was moved to do this. I as witness sense an alignment in myself that brings me to imagine that she was in alignment with her own thread as she did this. She took the action. What happened for the other mover? Was she disturbed by this? Did she feel intruded upon? Did it take her away from her own thread? Or was she receptive, able to include and be changed by the introduction of another energy, another flow into her thread?

I don't know as witness what is happening internally for either mover. But what I do know is that the turbaned mover leans in, and that now the two movers are joined in Violet. That what was two is now one and each is changed by the other and something new is formed. The turbaned mover had the option to turn away, to reject, to discern that this incoming energy is not for me, it will take me from the flow of my thread rather than add something. How does she know this? By feeling the question or the energy as it arrives or arises in her field. Does her body or heart or spirit welcome it? Does her body or heart or spirit have a place for it? As she pays attention to her inner witness, the energy that holds and observes without judgement, what is happening? Everything is allowed. What is arising? Through that she will discern, yes or no. Does my body tighten and contract? Does my body open or have a curiosity? What has Creation brought to me? Is it to add to my experience or is it a distraction? The body and heart will inform you. I belong here. This feels right. Not *good* necessarily, but *right*.

In life, it is common to fall asleep and lose the path or to be called away and get lost. Sometimes the path is dark and brambly, sometimes clear as a blue sky. Whether brambly and dark or clear and bright, it has a call, it has a sound, it has a color, a vibration that makes it recognizable to us. We know when we are on it, that it belongs to us and we know to be with it. We can yoke to our sacred paths. Aware, in the witness state, our paths are present.

Action

To take an action. To take an action with consciousness, with focus, with awareness. What a gift! Remember how wide the circle is, how wide the vastness of life is. To take an action is to choose or be chosen by a movement, a movement of the body, the mind, the heart, the soul. To put

something into physical form. Out of this vastness, I choose this, or I was chosen by this. Out of all possibilities, it is this that I choose. Here a mover finds a turquoise silk. I happen to know that this particular mover just came from time in Hawaii.

Is it happenstance that she chooses the color of Hawaiian waters? Or did the color call her to it? As she holds the silk, she is moved to work with it in a way that tosses the silk up and down, creating wave like movements, creating incredible shapes. The silk becomes extremely alive and active in this movement. As a witness, I feel in my own body as though she is bringing in the energy of the ocean, the unpredictability, the beauty and the embrace of the ocean. The shape that cannot be caught, cannot stay still, she is bringing in the tides and through that the moon. I am connected to the heavens through this movement. She embodied the action. She connected with the silk and listened to how the silk and her body wanted to interact, wanted to move and then she embodied it. It began a conversation between herself and the silk. As a mover, she does not see what I see as the witness. Her experience of the movement is internal. We each are in the presence of mystery and each in a different way. She does not know how this appears to the outside world. I do not know what she is experiencing inwardly, what the conversation is between her and the silk.

It is like in Life. We make our movements, take our actions. If we are aware, conscious, we are in a conversation with our actions and the fruit of that action. We do not know everything there is to know. The mystery is still present, but again, we feel the rightness of our places, of our actions and what we have been shown or urged to do.

Mystery

And then there is the darkness, what we do not see, what we do not know, what is hidden or unconscious, what is held by the mystery. The mystery can be welcomed into your life. Can you be content with the Not Knowing? Or if not content, then at least accepting the relationship? Can you accept that there is a greater source called mystery that one cannot possibly know in the way of conscious thought, conscious understanding? It is too big for us.

Can this be all right? For me, I sense an enormous dark warmth enveloping me with love. I sense a brilliant white light enveloping me with love. It is mysterious and true.

I allow this to be enough. Along with our consciousness, our awareness, the gifts of beauty that the world constantly offers to us as encouragement to live, can we quiet our thirst to know enough to be content with life and to live it fully? Or with our insatiable thirst to know, can we ride it and ride it, knowing through it a bit more and a bit more and a bit more of what it is we seek, but still not be stopped in it by becoming jammed up in the mind? The mind always wants to know. That's what the mind does. Appease the mind, let it seek its answers. Let the seeking be part of the roadmap, but not the whole thing.

We are more than the seeking. For if we are always in the seeking mode, we do not realize that we are already here, already whole, already enough. We are each enough. Now. We do not need One More Thing. We have enough. Now. One mover runs in circles, around and around the space. She is circling the whole. Another mover with wrapped head has arms extended and forearms pointed down. Her knees are slightly bent, she is dancing to an inner rhythm. She is entering other worlds that she inhabits through these movements. A third mover has her hands on her abdomen. As a witness I am taken into her interiority. A fourth mover is at the pole, the Tree of Life. She has a purple silk over her head, she is possibly in conversation with the beings who advise her, a fifth mover is barely visible behind the post. Her movement is hidden, cloaked, unseeable in this moment.

Each one of these movers is enough. I could witness just one of them all day, and that mover would be enough. Together, they are enough. They are each deeply engaged with their own current, their own thread. They do not know what is happening around them, except through what they can sense, what they can intuit and what is being told to them internally by the presence who guides them. They each know enough. The field is very active and even for those who can visibly see and witness there is a Not Knowing present. The Not Knowing Energy, when you can really feel it, and the quality of love and ecstasy it carries is the Grace. It is the gift itself.

You can ride it, you can be in it, you can let it move you, you can share it, you can be flooded by it, but you cannot own it, you cannot dominate it, you cannot win it. It is not for sale. You cannot possess it. Can this be enough? Enough to form good relationships, to do good deeds, to make good plans, to set your course, to discern your actions? We each have authority over our lives in co-creation with divine energy, the result can be deeply satisfying, deeply successful, not in a material sense, but in the way of who we deeply are being realized.

Holding the Inner Stillness

There is movement and there is stillness. There is action and there is pause. This is true in the circle. This is true in life. In the action we have been moved, we have been called, urged, taken. We are in a flow of making things happen, bringing about creation, activity. We are moving energy. Life is changing around us as a result of what we are doing. If we are in touch with that inner calling, it feels good and right. We feel supported by the unseen, by the invisible. What we are doing is ours to do.

And then the action is complete, maybe for now, maybe forever. Its energy is spent. The fuel it had is gone and a result is present. The result may be immediately known by us. If the movement was a painting, the painting is now there before us. If the movement was to clean your house, your house is now clean. If the movement was to start a school, the school is now up and running. In the movement circle, it is less concrete. You follow a tightness in your belly. It leads you into a wild dance that takes over your body. You follow a sensation in your throat and chest. It leads you into sobbing or singing. You are following your thread.

Eventually, the thread slackens. You lie down. You pause. You are in the Great Stillness. The Great Silence. Where there is all that is so profound and so complete, it can feel empty, like nothing.

To rest there, to simply *Be There* is a great gift. To have the invitation to enter that space of great stillness is an honor and affirmation of the holiness of life. The silence has a particular quality of richness, as though it is filled with light. For me, it feels as though it is filled with waves of moving light, teeming with a radiant, silent, sparkling sound. And to be in it, just being, is to be held in that light. The light of Silence, the Light of Non-Doing.

We often do not recognize it. In our world, we are busy, very connected to Doing, to Action. We do not honor or even recognize space and Stillness and Silence. If we do not recognize it, we certainly are not benefitting from it. We are not being filled by it. Authentic Movement as a practice teaches this. It teaches both the Movers and the Witnesses to recognize and to honor the Stillness and the Silence as a place, as a movement of its own. The Stillness is like a Great Embrace of Light or, if you will, of Darkness. Nothing is happening. We simply are breathing in and out. Our minds are quiet. Our hearts are quiet, our bodies are quiet. There is no chatter. We can hear now. We can hear the Silence. We can hear the inner winds. We can hear the fullness of creation, sometimes we can hear the gods speaking. It is palpable.

We have done enough for the moment. And the next action has not yet revealed itself. The energy for what is next has not yet gathered. We are on a holy break.

Patterns

Patterns can free us or can hold us in a locked constraint. I am in a new place, writing this book. Normally, I live in town. Now, I am out in the woods. I have no phone, no internet, no email, no car. I have what I brought. I find that I have brought far more than I need. More clothes than I need, more books, more files, more food. I find I need far less than I imagine. This is often so. I actually need very little. We don't need much to live and yet we surround ourselves with things. While many of these things are a distraction, some of them are not. Some of them are tools for living. Tools for going deep. Tools for living your thread, working with your thread, objects for expressing and supporting your nature. Those tools you need.

When I came here to the Northeast Kingdom and was dropped off, I had no patterns established. I am without what I know. I am without the rhythm of my normal life, without my patterns. This is good. This is what I wanted. This is what I knew I needed to write this book. I was disoriented. I begin to write, my primary focus for coming. As I write, rhythm begins to form around me, to rise up out of the primary activity. I write and I need a break. I write and I am tired. I write and I need exercise, I write and I am hungry. For the first day, it is new, for the second it feels familiar, for the third day, it feels like a welcome pattern, a welcome rhythm. I am walking outside at dawn, the sun is rising. It is 3 below zero. Three below zero at sunrise in the snow looks a certain way. Magnificent color spreads everywhere, crystalline beauty. Frost shines. Air sparkles. The sound of footsteps crunch. The trees crack and pop in the cold.

I think, I want to see this tomorrow, I want to see this again. I notice the time and I know that it is possible for me to see this again tomorrow, God willing, if I come outside at the same time or a bit earlier, if the sky is clear, if a sunrise is visible. It is possible because the earth has a rhythm, the sunrise has a rhythm, there is a pattern to the rising and setting of the sun. It is predictable and my body operates within it. I rise by it and go to sleep by it. The seasons turn outside and within me. My heart beats in a rhythm, my arterial blood pumps in a rhythm, my venous blood pumps in another rhythm, my cranial fluid pumps in yet another. There are rhythms in life, of life that hold it together, that keep it going, that actually are intrinsic to life existing. Life is rhythm and life is music in that way. We are affected by these patterns, we are in these patterns, through no effort of our own. Through tuning into them we can access the cosmic.

What happens; however, in many of us, is that we fill up with patterns that are not part of this natural rhythm of living. We do things in a certain way because when we started that action, it felt right but soon, it went on automatic. More and more becomes automatic. When we get up in the morning, we automatically reach for coffee, for tea, sit down, look at a computer, turn on the radio, whatever it is rather than being conscious and aware of what we are doing. Then the pattern is ruling us. Soon we are addicted to our patterns. They fill and dictate our lives. We drink or eat to soothe depression. We distract ourselves with endless information and entertainment to soothe anxiety rather than simply being awake to the moment of life. We are not in our authority. It is difficult to be released from this. These patterns are a closed circuit. They go around and around and around. They repeat. Nothing new can come in. There is no room, no space for authenticity.

This is even true down to a physical level. We walk the same route to work. We run the same path for exercise, shop at the same time each week. Around and around and around. Our bodies become habituated and locked into these patterns. Our bodies shape themselves around the habits we have. This can be helpful or harmful. What it doesn't allow for is novelty or creation or holiness to act. We can't hear, we can't see. We may be blinded by our own habits and patterns. Holiness is speaking to us and we cannot hear or see it.

In Authentic Movement, this manifests as being a cyclical pattern of movement that does not have a thread. A thread is something you can hold and follow, it has a movement that goes somewhere. A closed system of pure pattern does not.

Once, when practicing in a week long Authentic Movement retreat when my movements went very deep, I had the experience of many automatic patterns in me being if not erased, then being overridden to such an extent that they were not in operation when I came home. I did not notice it while at the retreat, but the next morning at home, when I went to make my daughter pancakes for breakfast, something I had done hundreds of times before, there was no Pancake Pattern in me. I had not forgotten how to make pancakes, but I did not automatically reach for the ingredients. I did not automatically do what I had done hundreds of times before. Now every step was consciously chosen. Get the flour, the measuring cup, crack the egg, now stir. Every step was now chosen. I was awake with the pancakes. What was the quality of these pancakes I wonder? Did they taste better? Did they nourish her more, as more of my presence was there as I created them? I don't know, but certainly the experience of making the pancakes was a far richer one for me.

In practicing Authentic Movement, if we start with the thread that comes from our sensations, our bodies, our emotions, our imagination, our spirits, if we listen carefully into that silence without trying to fill it prematurely with a pattern just to make the Silence stop, just to make the stillness stop, because it scares us, makes us uneasy, we are in the flow, in the traveling.

We are not in a pattern that is closed. We are engaged with a open system. An open system allows, invites creativity. The doors are open, the pattern is not there or not dictating and something new, something from never before can enter, can come into existence, can become conscious. Isn't this exactly what we need?

Think of the world and the entrenchment of the patterns we have as human beings, some of them benign, some of them positive, and many of them destructive. Our oil consumption, for example, our water consumption, for example. These are patterns we have that cost a great price to the earth and ultimately to our own existence as well as the existence of all living things on this planet. We consume far more than we need. We are not conscious about what we are doing. It is comfortable for us to remain in our pattern of using far more than we need, even though it could cause our ultimate demise. That is how powerful the lack of awareness and willingness to directly engage is. It can kill us and the whole planet and some of us are okay with that. We have patterns of violence of all kinds from the most subtle meanness to the most overt horrendous displays of cruelty. It is rare for the participants in the violence to listen into the Stillness long enough to find the thread that will lead them out of it, out of the closed circle.

But some of us are not okay with this. Collectively our consciousness, through men, women, children, plants and animals is steadfastly working to become freed from patterns that bind us to destructive living. Many people are consciously awake to what can be done. Nelson Mandela was one man who did exactly that and look at the good that happened through him. How many more Nelsons do we have? Many. Let's open our eyes. Nelson Mandela created his life through listening inwardly and following his thread. We can all do this. Am I a Nelson? Are you? Who are you with your thread?

The Goodness of Patterns, the Goodness of Rhythm

All patterns are not destructive. We need them. Not everything requires our full attention. We have the kind of minds and brains that can remember, store, and draw upon what has been learned or known before. This is extremely valuable and the extent to which we can do this means that we don't have to keep reinventing the wheel. I can tie my shoe automatically, giving it little attention. My muscle memory knows how to do it. I can drive a car, with a lot of it being automatic. My muscle memory, my experience, my knowledge of the terrain all make it so that I do not need to be on high alert when driving, simply alert to changes. I don't have to think about everything as though it were new. I can rely on what I know to take me where I need to go today,

In the Authentic Movement practice, in myself and in other movers, I feel and I witness how some patterns can actually take people deeper. With myself, when I move, I often notice that when a movement begins in me, if I give myself over to the repetition of the movement, the repetition of the pattern, it opens into a flow that moves on its own accord. I am riding it, allowing it, letting my body be the instrument of the movement. With one mover I have witnessed for years, she frequently covers her head, she begins a dance I have seen many times, the dance has a particular quality and pattern, the dance opens up then to a space that is new each time, she receives communication here, someone or something speaks to her here. Still another mover peers down into the earth for long periods of time, each time however, she receives something different. These patterns are actually doorways to the holy. Doorways to the sacred. They are part of the familiar path we each travel in our own particular Spirit to access the holy. They take us to our *sit spot*, the place inside where we go to cultivate quiet mind, where we wait to be called, to be seen, by the invisible. These patterns are like the rituals in a Catholic

Mass, or the rituals in an indigenous sacred ceremony. They are not the end, and when practiced with awareness, they are a helpful map to get to the holy land.

It is like the patterns or rhythms before bed, especially important for the child, but even as adults, we have them. To go to sleep is a huge event, to close one's eyes, to say goodbye to the day, to give oneself over to the blackness of night and to the light of the stars, is a big deal. This day is over. I am shutting down everything willful now. I put on my pajamas, have a snack, brush my teeth, hear a story, have a lullaby. This prepares me, this ritual prepares me for what I am about to do: give my trust to the darkness, to the night, to the stars, to hand over my will.

We have similar movement rituals in the Authentic Movement practice. For each person, they are unique. For each person it is an inner discovery. The rituals are not the same for anyone, even if they look the same. These patterns are very helpful, like rising of the sun, the turning of the seasons, the repetition of the heart's beat. To witness these patterns as they are occurring changes them from being asleep to being aware. You are not caught in them, you are riding with them.

A surfer would say, in order to surf, I must wax my board, get my proper gear on, wade out into the water, get on my board and paddle out, wait for wave, catch the wave at the right time. Then I surf. I am with the wave, the wave and I are having an experience of each other, and sometimes the door to oneness opens.

In Authentic Movement practice, we see that energy spreads. We see that energy is connected, that there is a web. We see that we are communicators and that we are relational beings. We see that what one person does affects everyone, whether directly or indirectly. When

a mover spreads out the gold cloth, when she takes the time to make that path, what was empty before she did it now has a road. That path belongs to everyone in the circle. We all now have that thread to follow energetically, mystically, spiritually, because that one mover knew to do it.

We don't have to do it all. We don't have to sacrifice ourselves. We just have to do our part. To do, as my friend Beth Hin says, our portion. To take our portion, to act our portion. It is not too much. As Baby Bear says, "It is just right." It rings actually with joy.

Holy Woman, Holy Man

Holiness is everywhere.

I know a holy woman who tattoos her body, smokes pot, eats meat, drinks beer, and dresses in vibrant crazy colors.

I know a holy man who drives a truck and lives in the woods and keeps to himself, quietly offering assistance when needed.

I know a holy woman who offers her mind and heart to the world, who works really hard to educate and enlighten the mind and action of people on behalf of the green world.

I know a holy man who is a business man, who deals in high stakes, with fast moving business people. I give thanks every day that he is where he is doing what he is doing, bringing his heart to that world.

I know a holy woman who runs a small store, who struggles and rises up, day after day after day. She struggles and rises up for all of us. She does not stay down. Ever. Not ever

I know a holy man who exudes friendliness, unassumingness, who graces the town he lives in simply through his presence. He remembers something essential of primary goodness and to be in his presence, you remember this also.

I know a holy woman who became a holy man.

I know a holy woman who honors silence and mystery so deeply and fully I am inspired by her daily dance with it.

I know a holy man who struggles with alcoholism and drug addiction -- who every day questions his life, its meaning, and whose life causes others to question it as well.

I know a holy woman who goes to church twice a day, every day, no matter what and who spends the moments she is not in church being the church as she lives her daily life.

I know a holy man who delivers mail, greets people, gives dogs treats.

I know a holy child who surfs and fishes and spreads love through his joy.

I know a holy woman who attends daily to great depth and great faith and a great creativity, who travels subtleties, who listens to the silence, who dances and paints, and tells the truth when she speaks.

I know a holy child who builds sand castles and rides his bike and loves his big brother.

I know a holy man who makes everyone laugh.

I know another holy man who is dead serious.

The holiness shines through, shines through. I live among holy beings.

I am graced by their light. The world is graced by their presence.

The world is graced by your presence.

Helpers from the Unseen World

As I write this book, different helpers from the unseen world are appearing to assist me, to inform me, and to hold me. Here in the Northeast Kingdom where I write, the raven has appeared. She flies in, out and around, each day, talking to me. The owl has shown up, sweeping with its soft and silent wings. On the inner planes, a conscious baby has shown up—a wise infant who puts a hand on my cheek and speaks to me deeply and with great compassion. I feel as though I am in the presence of a great gift. I spoke earlier of the Flower of Life and how it is accompanying me on this journey, shining and illuminating.

During a movement session many years ago when I had travelled to a state of being very distant from my physical body, I was guided back by angelic beings who showed up and tended to me. I named them the Angels of the In-Between. They are pure love, always there, and exist in the space between all things. As I go to sleep, asking for guidance on this book, the Angels of the In-Between return in my dream showing me through the colors of a very soft green and a very soft blue that love is the matrix we exist in. Love is the matrix we exist in. We are never alone, we are never without it.

I am to convey that working with Authentic Movement and the embodied prayers are in alignment with the resonance of the infinite. The prayers as they are conceived, embodied, received, moved are resonating out like the Flower of Life. I am to convey that the work is vast. The vibration of Color and its support of the movement and the prayers are bringing in a pure dimension of Beauty as an offering and as a guide. This is enormously helpful and important. The colors go directly into and with what wants to be moved with no agenda, no dogma, no words, no ideas, just pure vibration. The colors travel easily.

131

The imaginative experiences I had with Color as a child are actually occurring here in the circle. There are a certain number and color of the silks in the room, but the actuality is that the whole space fills with color and the colors are active movers on the mystical plane. I am to speak of how this work is so much more than it appears on the surface, both on an individual level, a collective level, and a universal level. The Stillness is full and potent. We all have dreams for our lives. My dream is that we each can approach and taste the dreams that burn in us. I did not know this so clearly until I began to write this book.

My deepest dream is for humanity's rich joy and true awareness. Authentic Movement is simply one pathway to the deep connection that supports the kind of inner knowing and inner action and relationship to creativity and embodiment of that creativity that can bring about joyful living and experience of the Interconnected Web that we are. The possibilities are limitless. The imagination has free reign here and the imagination creates.

Creation is the fingerprint of the Holy.

Simple Joyful Living

When she took the bread from the oven the brown crusty top had the hollow sound when tapped. The scent filled the house. And her family was waiting to slice into it.

When he was able to complete the job, with all loose ends tied up and feel it was his best work.

When we all do our best work and we know it inside.

When she saw the devastation of her flooded neighborhood and then heard the sound of her father's voice who had arrived to help her.

When she had that one afternoon in the hemlock grove in the winter. Blue sky. Sun shone and when the wind blew the snow off the trees, the sparkle flew into the air.

When she lost the sense of time as she painted and the colors took her.

When he lost the sense of time as he wrote and the words took him.

When she could swim in the ocean and there was no place else she had to go.

When as he climbed the mountain, he realized it didn't matter if he reached the top.

When they reached the top of the mountain and could see all-around, all directions.

When they got caught in the hailstorm in July and ran through the ice pellets and lightning, laughing.

When the horse ran up to him in recognition and anticipation.

When the dog followed her everywhere, eyes watching every move.

When the birdsong woke her and she listened for 15 minutes before getting up.

When the stranger's smile reminded him of some long forgotten place inside.

When all alone, because you want to be.

When surrounded by people because you want to be.

When playing music or singing a song and the notes are exactly right.

When the beginning promise of the day enters in and can be ridden until nightfall.

When night falls and you are glad for the rest.

When the night holds you well.

When her direction is on course and she can feel that.

When he can sense the bigger picture.

When she knows she is not alone, even when by herself.

That day her dream came true.

When they resolved the argument and then laughed.

When they resolved the argument and remembered their love.

When he had a sudden insight that made everything make more sense.

When the coffee was just perfect.

When she waved goodbye from the doorway and you could see the image in your mind's eye for years later.

When we trusted the course of things and saw all sides, and focused on the best.

When she felt the openness of possibility.

When the sun rose again the next morning,

When the stars came out and we could see them so clearly.

The Mist: Bridging the Two Worlds—Returning with Your Treasure

The Lady of the Lake emerges from the mist and returns to the mist. Did I see her? Was she ever there? Was it a mirage? A dream? Did I even have a dream? I can't recall. Let's have some tea. The kettle is put on, the tea is brewed and the experience is lost. The experiences of the Mist are delicate, like gossamer. If we come at them with a heavy-handed mind, they vanish. Often, we do not dwell in the space they come from long enough. We do not allow for how time moves in the openness of that space to reach us. Time is fluid, time is misty, depending upon the plane of consciousness we are operating from, we perceive time differently. If you have been traveling through Misty places, allow time to come into resonance with where you are now. You have permission to allow time and space to find the rhythm with each other that may possibly allow you to remember or stay connected and integrated with the inner teachings that come to you like jewels, like dreams, beyond the veil.

As we interact with the mist, with the mystical, it can be so alive when we are there in the experience. Then as we open our eyes, and see the day world, it fades or vanishes or seems inconsequential or unreal in this very concrete world we have here. Language is a poor translator.

Through awareness, awareness of your physical body, and what may be activated and anchoring there, and also awareness of the more subtle energies within you and around you, it is possible to stay with this bridge. Often mystical experiences are perceived through these more subtle bodies and as we allow the time and space to stay with the experience until it anchors into the density of the physical, we are more apt to not lose it. It can be likened perhaps to the tortoise and the hare. If the hare is the mystical experience, if we can pause with that until the tortoise of the physical time and space can catch up and anchor into it, then there remains a link, a memory and knowing of the swift hare before it runs off.

I am a deep traveler of the Mists. I trust them fully. I go back and forth. I feel that we are now in a time where it is much more possible for the mystical experiences and energies to be more fully part of our waking state. The density of living is shifting to higher and lighter frequencies.

After the bell rings to close the circle, everyone is full. Each participant is in a different deep state of awareness, of emotionality, of what has opened in their bodies, in the worlds they traveled on the inner planes. One person may have been moving and relating to their bones, their skeletal structure. Another person may have been in deep conversation with mystical colors and geometry, still another was traveling to an indigenous medicine man or woman and receiving instruction or healing, still another may have been exploring childhood trauma. Another person may have been witnessing for a long time and is holding all that he or she has received as the witness, others experiences, and their own. The time is crucial and potent. How do we integrate what has occurred? First by deeply honoring that something, however ineffable, has occurred. And if you have been tracking and awake, your body remembers where it has been, remembers what has happened. When I use the word body, I am referring not only to the physical self but to the many dimensions of the energy field.

As human beings, in spite of our huge brains and vast capacities to create and act, many of us have a hard time remembering. It is important when the bell gently sounds the end of a session and we are in the state of transition from one place to another, to honor that the movements that were occurring with eyes closed or from the Witness state are still moving. Nothing has stopped. The movements are happening on many planes of consciousness and just because the bell rang and the eyes are now open, does not mean that the movements have concluded. Your body has apparently stopped, but the movement is still occurring. Some of the movements, depending upon their nature, will move for a very long time. Some of them that are connected to the infinite will move indefinitely. It is important to realize that as a Mover and as a Witness you are now different. You are not who you were when you first closed your eyes. You are welcoming back a different self.

Even though language is clumsy, it can be a surprisingly effective vehicle for bridging the world of the mist, weaving it into the Day world. What threads did you find this time? Is it important for you to communicate? Does what you have just moved have an urgency inside of you to be shared or brought back in some way? Either through your own private writing or drawing or through speaking or gesturing in the offering circle? Give time and attention to what you feel in your body during this transitional time. Honor that if there is an urge to speak, the words will show up. Remember that you have been tracking, you have had an inner witness the entire time who has been there and seen and felt everything. A quiet time of transition for reflection can facilitate the integration of the depth of the experience, giving voice to the inarticulate.

As you tune into your body and allow the words or gestures to arise, they themselves have the vibration of the story or the experience. They will unfold. Sometimes your story is important to tell for your own development of your soul. Sometimes it is important to tell, not for you, but because someone else needs to hear it. Remember that we are all connected. When the movers begin to speak, what is revealed often is the deep level of synchronicity that was happening.

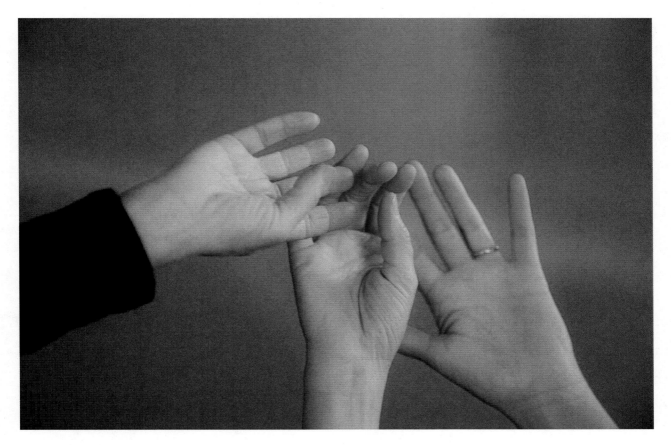

There were certain elements, themes, beings that appeared not for just one mover, but for two, for three, for all. We begin to see that the Mists surround us all like a great cloak and we are indeed not lonely travelers although we are certainly unique travelers. We see that all the journeys are respected and important.

Speaking, Language, Giving Voice

At the end of each session we move into an offering circle. In the offering circle, with the tenderness of the fresh experience, at times it is important to let the movement sit without words defining it in any way. At other times, it is beneficial to bring language and voice to the experience.

When we allow language to arise out of the fresh experience, we are marking the experience in the conscious world. We are inviting it to sit at the table of being recognized and seen, of being witnessed and valued. I believe that even though our words can never be precise enough to capture the layered subtleties of the experience, attempting to come close to it through giving voice to it, helps to create that inner bridge between the worlds.

Giving language, however clumsy or seemingly partial, begins to create in each of us our own bilingual vocabulary. What is the language of our inner and deepest world? To begin to know it through practice allows that part of ourselves to take a stronger place in the living of our lives. Rather than being always in the shadow, we give it voice.

We are thereby enriched. In the offering circle, no one comments or questions what you say. It is assumed and known that you are the authority of your own experience and that what you say is what happened. This helps people to heal that wound that so many of us have of being questioned and doubted, undermined, and diminished. The time of the offering circle is often one of immense beauty. As the silences are honored as much as the words and gestures, as the naturalness of each person's language is given space and voice. As the gifts that were accessed and were given from the Mists find their place in the Day world and hence become a conscious part of us. We own what just happened.

This becomes a bridge into living authentically, honoring the depth that spurs our actions, our decisions, our relationships. Our roots are deep and many forces of the invisible are constantly working with us. The Mist is always here. It allows us to more deeply trust the actions we take, even if we cannot explain them in rational terms. We can stand in our place with what we know. We can trust our capacity to communicate, trust that the words will be there when we connect to the feeling or the sense or the energy. We become speakers of a certain kind of truth, words that are not weapons, that have no hidden agenda, that are not defended or defensive. We become instruments beyond the Weapon, beyond Duality, beyond War and Peace, yet deeply connected to our Sacred Signatures.

I began teaching Authentic Movement over 20 years ago. I have a healing practice that is constantly evolving, as I evolve. Many people have asked me over the years to teach them how to do what I do. While I could teach certain methods, I could teach them the kind of body work I practice or I could teach them kinesiology or sound healing as I practice it or energy work as I practice it, I could not teach them what it was they were really asking for. There is no method for that. I am not *doing* anything in particular. I am not following anything but the person who comes to me for help or guidance. That is the method I am following. That is what I am moving with. I did not want people to follow in my footsteps with a methodology. The methodology is not the key. Anything can bring about desired or needed change if the attention, focus, and space are given to it. The best way I knew to teach this was through the practice of Authentic Movement. Here I knew that people would be put in touch with their own guidance, their own rhythms, their own natural ways. It would not be about me, but about them, and how the Holy works through them. That is why I began to teach this practice to others.

Always the roots, I see now, were to spread the possibility for all who have studied with me to understand their subterranean rivers and to feel the support and guidance from the Mists, from the Invisible, from the Holy, to not get lost there, and to know how to use and integrate what they find.

Holiness, Prayer, and Softness

To enter the space and experience of the holy can take you to your knees. Although it can be as smooth as the surface of a glacial lake, it is full of the awe that that glacial lake is and inspires. To enter the relationship and domain of the holy is to surrender to mingling with the mystery of it, the creative constancy of it; it is to be willing to be changed. Right then and there. Holiness can be serene and it can also be a mighty force to reckon with. Complacency does not survive in the presence of the holy.

How does holiness speak to you?

In my world, prayer is a constant act moving from my heart and breath. My prayer is my conversation, my daily living. I am not thinking about it, nor does it often have words. At certain times; however, I focus the energy of this with a ceremony that brings in a particular movement of intention or question. I ask God, the Divine, Creation for attention to a particular question. That question may be personal or very vast. It involves a place in my awareness where something feels as though it needs to move and it is not moving, not flowing.

Direct Knowing

As we navigate our lives, we come to trust certain people. Life brings us treasures in the form of other human beings. We can deeply feel and sense when a person is important to us. There is a resonance, a ringing, a shininess to the connection. We can feel deep parts of who we are stirred and intensified. These are soul connections. The network of these connections works in conjunction with the Great Mystery, keeping us on our paths, allowing points of illumination. We can give and take from these beings pieces of their wisdom, their sage advice, what they have learned along the way, and they in return can receive from us.

We can also experience the gift of direct knowing, those moments when there is apparently no intercessor. We have moments in our lives when we simply and fully know something. We haven't heard it necessarily or read it, we just know it. These moments can happen while moving and while living. In Authentic Movement, in the open space of the great mysterious circle, through the embodiment, the cells of our bodies, the energies of our auras and chakras may simply open in such a way that we become in touch with knowing, a place where no doubt is present, where the thinking mind is not in control or necessary. We are in a place of oneness, where we simply *Are* and in the beingness of that, we *Know*. This does not happen because of

Authentic Movement. However, Authentic Movement can offer a discipline that facilitates the state of presence allowing it to be more possible. The experience of direct knowing is a spiritual elixir and affirming conversation with the Divine. It brings forward the essence of direct relationship with divinity.

Softness

I have spoken deeply here of being awake and aware. This awareness can be like a bolt of lightning, but can also come softly like the glow of a candle. It may be possible for humanity's awakening to come through gentleness and softness, through letting go. What if everyone had an awareness within themselves of how they were holding tension, physical, emotional, and mental tension and could through the simplicity of the question, "What could be lighter? What could be even lighter than that?" release that tension. The simple asking of the question and the awareness brought to the space that follows the question brings a level of peace. It is not dissimilar to speaking to God. The prayer is made, then attention given to the space that follows. Rather than filling that space up with yourself, try honoring the space, allowing the space before you to just be. See what answers you back.

Feelings transmit. A feeling of harshness will transmit and tighten things up. Alternatively, a feeling of softness, of invitation to lightness can also be transmitted and can introduce a new idea, a new way of thinking, feeling, moving, being. As in Authentic Movement, as in Prayer, as in Awareness in Life, we can bring softness in and everything can change.

In my neck, what would happen if I let go of my shoulder, if I were lighter in my shoulders? My neck softens, remembers itself. How do I hold my neck and shoulders when I am in an argument with my friend, child, colleague, or spouse? I bring in the question, through awareness, how can this be lighter? What can I let go of here, loosen up on? What if I simply started to breathe more deeply? What would that do? What if I loosened my shoulders or unlocked my knees? What would happen then to the argument? What if I lowered my voice or softened my eyes? What would happen if I simply touched the person with whom I argue on the arm in real connection, just for a moment. What would that do?

Awareness does not have to be harsh, like a brilliant glare. It can be soft, soft as the glow of burning ember.

My life is modest and deeply fulfilling. I am graced and in the flow of life. I have co-created what I have through the pathway of listening and following my spirit, trusting deeply in the gifts that I am graced with, from my inner qualities to the people and events that enter my life. I consider everything that comes my way as an expression of the Divine. Is this mine to work with or do I let this continue on in the flow? It is this work that makes a life. That is what I am here to do.

And the White Stones

About 25 years ago, after the stones had been sitting in their copper bowls with turquoise enamel center, they began to speak to me. They told me that they wanted to be used ceremonially from this point forward. They showed me that they wanted to be cleared (perhaps of the grief) and how to do that. They showed me that they wanted to be wrapped in a silk cloth. They showed me that the first time I was to use them ceremonially was in a sound ceremony that I was to do with a deep friend and mentor who was at a landmark in her life.

From this point forward the White Stones have worked with me ceremonially. They are no longer grief stones, but an intrinsic part of my ceremonial work. They are present with the Authentic Movement groups, as they work in ceremony, either outwardly or behind the scenes, and with my work in other ways. They are here with me now as I write.

They have been out during this entire time, under the stars, forming a medicine wheel, holding space. They are right now, covered in snow.

Soon I will gather them, wrap them back up in their silk, and offer a prayer of thanksgiving.

We are never alone, even when we feel most alone, we are not alone. Some of us have lives that seem easy on the outside, but inwardly may be rife with challenges. Others of us have lives that are outwardly difficult, sometimes horrendous, and possibly inwardly rewarding in unexpected ways. We don't get to dictate every aspect of our lives. We get to do some of that. So much of life is living with what is given to us, no matter how easy or difficult.

To be able to be within the complex fabric of your own life whether that life is high in the mountains as a hermit or in the fast-paced world of modern society or in a war-torn environment. You are where you are. We are where we are. This is it. This is what we have. Right here. In this moment. We are who we are, where we are, how we are, when we are.

And to be in that with the deepest possible capacity to know and to trust oneself, and one's inner connection with what is called the Inner Witness, Holiness, Higher Self, Deep Intuition, God, Inner Spirit, True Self, makes it doable, possible and sometimes joyful. The joy is not necessarily because the circumstance is an uplifting one, but because the inner connection is open and flowing and transmitting information, knowledge, and guidance. We are not alone.

I realize as I conclude this book that I am writing about being human, which seems peculiar. We are humans, why would we need any guidance at all? And yet, I experience that so many of us do. It is not easy to live this life. We struggle with it in ways that other species do not seem to.

It is my hope and my prayer that what is divinely human in each of us comes into full flower.

Whether our lives are easy or difficult, rich or poor, healthy or sick, may we each find our way. We are not alone. We are connected, interconnected, to each other, known and unknown. We are larger than ourselves.

We are a massive, pulsing, Authentic Movement circle, that includes all humans, all animals, all plants, all mountains, all lakes, all oceans, all rivers, all prairies, all jungles, all deserts, all cities, all farms, all temples, all mosques, all churches, all monasteries, all kivas, all prisons, all war zones, all ravaged lands, all pollution, all inventions, all hopes, all discoveries, all new thinking, all new ways, all stars, all planets, all beings everywhere.

May we each find our place. May we make room for each other. May we witness the light and the darkness in each other.

We are all here. This is what we have. We are not alone.

Harmony is possible.

May we allow it to be so.

May we find it.

May we not stop moving until we find it.

Until we come to that collective Holy Pause

And Exhale.

From The Mists

I rise up and out
It is time for
What could not be seen and known
in the hearts of people
to find its place of belonging.
I am here for this
for all of humanity
to find its place of belonging
For the earth and her inhabitants
to find the mutual song.
I offer all the gifts I know
for this
for the song to be fully sung.
In the Mists
There is a healing realm
All Souls are welcome.
The light and sound find and match
exactly what the soul needs.
It lives within us
this place of healing waters
of healing mists.
In my dream now
the war is over.

My grandmother is at rest.

As I walk the fields now,

the war torn places have grown over.

Plants grow the landscape into green

New species rise up.

Plants, animals, and earth all speak together.

I can see where all weapons have been collected.

A group of people who see with new eyes

dismantle the weapons

bit by bit

Some materials are returned to the earth

Some are being reinvented.

I see new alliances

I see the impossible occurring

there are no weapons anywhere.

I see every one finds their place

Everyone knows where they belong

In the harmony the earth spins and glows

The earth sings

April, 2016

Acknowledgments

I extend my gratitude to the many without whom none of this would have happened:

To my family, Steve Pitonyak and Alexandra Sandman-Pitonyak.

To Elizabeth Anne Hin, whose teachings and friendship have guided me beyond measure.

To Sara Norton, who introduced me to this form and with whom I explore the mysteries.

To Barbara Crowe who cheers me on from the heavens.

To Janet Adler for her wisdom and teaching regarding this form.

To my dedicated early readers, whose attention, witnessing, editorial suggestions, and guidance have literally allowed me to continue: Ann Armbrecht, Kelley Hunter, Cynthia Kirkwood, Margo MacLeod, and Sara Norton.

To the leaderful groups: Eileen Chodos, Nancy Dennett, Tema Fishbein, Jesse Geller, Julie Leavitt, Jonathon Levin, Diana Levy, Emma Linderman, Julie Miller, Sue Millen, Sandy Muniz, Sara Norton, Marsha Kalina Perlmutter, Jody Platner, Shakti Sadeh, Susan Schell, Julia Shiang, Anne Smith, Sox Sperry, Lisa Tsetse, Jen Auletta, Hannah Dennison, Steffi Lahar, Peter Lawrence, Bonnie Morrisey.

To all who have participated in my groups studying this mystery with me, in particular: Jessie Alfarone, Ann Armbrecht,* Katie Back, Angie Barger,* Devon Beyers, MaryKay Blouin, Carol Charles, Liva Coe, Kelly Fairchild, Donna Goldberg, Amy Goodman, Kelley Hunter, Abbi Jaffe, AnneMarie John, Pam Kentish,* Cynthia Kirkwood,* Chris LaBruciano, Louise Low,* Lisa Mase, Emily Medley,* Lydia Russell, Candice Shaffer, Sarah Shapiro, Rachel Shea*, Nina Shoenthal, Susie Atwood Stone, Stefi Tucker, Avi Waring, Ulrike Wasmus,* Jeanie Williams, Kristina Wium, Kerrie Workman, Peter Young and all the many others whose movements and witnessing have become part of the fabric of this book and of me.

To Victoria Fraser, whose attention to the sacred in all things, entered my life at the perfect time, to become a unique unmistakable thread of spiritual integrity.

To Michael Pitonyak, who lent me use of his cabin in the woods, where this book was birthed.

To Henry Romaine, who attended to my well-being.

To Sarla Matsumura who edited, designed, and composed this book.

And to Barrie Fisher, with her great skill and artistry as a photographer.

*Photographs included with permission.

About the Author

Jan Sandman is a body, mind, heart, and spirit educator and guide. She is an Authentic Movement teacher, a certified Trager© Practitioner, sound healer, and Family Constellation facilitator. For more than 30 years, she has maintained a private practice, guiding people individually to become more connected physically, emotionally and spiritually with their deepest selves. She works with groups as a facilitator of Authentic Movement, both nationally and internationally, and also leads workshops in Family Constellations and Ceremonial Sound Healing. An artist and writer, Jan has published short stories, poems, and essays in various literary journals and collections, including *Authentic Movement: Moving the Body, Moving the Self; Being Moved, Volume Two*, edited by Patrizia Pallaro; and *A Moving Journal: Ongoing Expressions of Authentic Movement*. She was recently a guest speaker on the *Cosmic Inspiration* radio show, hosted by internationally known author and astromythologist, M. Kelley Hunter on the "Amazing Women of Power" station. For Jan, the core of her life is a connection to spirit that is grounded in the beauty of everyday life. You can reach Jan Sandman at jansandman@comcast.net or through her website www.jansandman.com.

Made in the USA
Columbia, SC
13 May 2021